Give us bread
but give us roses

Give us bread but give us roses

Working women's consciousness in the United States, 1890 to the First World War

Sarah Eisenstein

Routledge & Kegan Paul
London, Boston, Melbourne and Henley

First published in 1983
by Routledge & Kegan Paul plc
39 Store Street, London WC1E 7DD,
9 Park Street, Boston, Mass. 02108, USA,
296 Beaconsfield Parade, Middle Park,
Melbourne, 3206, Australia, and
Broadway House, Newtown Road,
Henley-on-Thames, Oxon RG9 1EN
Phototypeset by Input Typesetting Ltd, London
Printed in Great Britain by
T. J. Press, Padstow

Library of Congress Cataloging in Publication Data

Eisenstein, Sarah.

Give us bread but give us roses.
Bibliography: p.
Includes index.
1. Women—Employment—United States—History
Addresses, essays, lectures. I. Title.
HD6095.E35 1983   331.4'0973   83–4538

ISBN 0–7100–9479–5 (pbk.)

Contents

PART I

Introductory essays

Introduction

by Harold Benenson

In the 1890s and after in the United States the still prevalent Victorian conception of respectable womanhood excluded wage-earning women. In contemporary opinion the conditions of female factory labor in particular – the nature of the physical tasks, disregard for proper moral safeguards, and 'low companionship' – barred working-class women from attaining a truly feminine standard of social conduct. Yet wage-earning women themselves did not acquiesce in this judgment. Nor did they passively accept the harsh conditions which they confronted in unsafe factories and tenements. Their response to conservative social ideologies, and to their employment experience in the context of changing family relationships, was varied and complex. An analysis of the character and dynamics of this response has fundamental importance for social theories of women's consciousness.

It is this problem – the formation of consciousness among wage-earning women in a period of industrialization and expansion of women's employment (1890–1920) – which Sarah Eisenstein explores in *Give us Bread but Give us Roses: working women's consciousness in the United States, 1890 to the First World War*. Sarah Eisenstein began her research in 1969. In addition to using published sources, she combed organizational and personal archival collections that touched various aspects of the subject. These included materials on 'working girls' clubs and settlement house programs in the papers of Grace Dodge, the National Federation of Settlements, Hull House and other individual settlement houses,[1] records from the New York, Chicago and national Women's Trade Union

League,[2] the papers of working-class women organizers Leonora O'Reilly, Mary Kenney O'Sullivan, Agnes Nestor and Rose Schneiderman,[3] and documents on women of the Socialist Party and the Industrial Workers of the World.[4] Sarah Eisenstein proceeded on the basis of certain key assumptions: first, that the analysis of social consciousness could gain profoundly from the study of working-class women. And second, that major social changes, and the rise of female labor organization, and radical and feminist movements, in the pre-First World War era necessarily called into question elements of the existing sexual ideology. This period provided uniquely favorable conditions for the partial rejection of this ideology and assertion of an incipient group consciousness on the part of working women. The full plan of writing, generated by this research and initial perspective, was never completed because of Sarah Eisenstein's death in 1978. The essays which were left in final or draft form are collected in *Give us Bread but Give us Roses*. They are primarily concerned with describing working women's actual consciousness. But the following chapters also propose a specific approach to theoretical issues concerning the interaction between sexual and class cultures, dominant ideology and subordinate group experience, and industrialization and women's position in pre-industrial family and community environments.

Give us Bread but Give us Roses reconstructs the attitudes of a pioneer generation of young working women toward the conflicts engendered by their new experience of employment outside the home. These women were part of a female labor force of unprecedented size in the factories and stores of New York City, Philadelphia, Boston, Chicago and other cities. Those employed in the manufacturing industries of these centers were mainly, though not exclusively, of immigrant Jewish and Italian background.[5] Most held jobs between the ages of sixteen and twenty-five, before they married, and the vast majority still lived with their parents. Although these young women workers enjoyed a certain freedom by virtue of their wage-earning status and widened experience outside the home, they remained closely bound to their families by economic, cultural and emotional ties. The young women of this generation were among those who joined the 'Uprising' of thirty thousand shirtwaist makers (1909–10) and forged the first permanent labor organizations among women workers in the United States, in the garment trades. They were also affected by feminist political campaigns, supported by a broad range of middle-class women, and by socialist and syndicalist labor agitation.

These essays give expression to the rudimentary critique of degrading conditions of labor which working women articulated, and their claim to a womanly identity in the face of derogatory judgments to the contrary. In tracing the impact of changing work and family experience, sexual ideology and new conditions of women's self-awareness, the study develops a dialectical conception of the influences which shaped working women's consciousness. In two areas in particular, the relation of dominant to subordinate class cultures and the effects of industrialization on working women, *Give us Bread but Give us Roses* charts well-conceived lines of interpretation that avoid one-sided emphasis.

Regarding the first problem, the study examines the points of intersection and tension between a late Victorian, middle-class ideal of womanhood, and the actual experience and cultural background of working-class women. The restrictions of the Victorian ideal condemned the latter group to an unwomanly status. At the same time, working-class women were powerfully drawn to the image of marriage and home that originated in this same Victorian concept of sexual propriety preserved in woman's separate 'sphere.' *Give us Bread but Give us Roses* (and chapter 3 in particular) views this cultural domain as an arena of conflict, uneasy accommodation and especially, of 'negotiated response' on the part of working women to both dominant and critical feminist or working-class ideologies, in light of their own distinct experience. Working women's attitudes did not simply reflect either the dominant Victorian or alternative ideologies. Rather, they grew out of the women's active response both to new conditions of work and working-class life, and to the ideas which were available to them.

This approach avoids the simplifications of two popular historical treatments: the first, which focuses on the survival of the working-class family unit (and its centrality for women), tends to view working-class culture as fully separate, and working class women as unaffected by dominant social ideologies (for example, in work of Jane Humphries, or Louise A. Tilly and Joan W. Scott).[6] An opposing, equally one-sided emphasis is found in the many studies of nineteenth-century Victorian ideology of 'woman's sphere' which imply that this dominant mode of thought was the one operative cultural force affecting women of all classes. Unlike these historical approaches, the perspective of the present work permits a complex analysis of the relationships between dominant social ideology, and subordinate group experience and consciousness in the situation of working-class women.

The study develops a specific approach to a second arena of conflicting social and cultural forces as well. This concerns the relationship between the new industrial pursuits of wage-earning women and their continued involvement in traditional family and community roles which were rooted in pre-industrial immigrant cultures. *Give us Bread but Give us Roses* (especially chapter 5) suggests that the break with traditional family obligations and community ways of life was not as sharp, in the case of newly employed working women, as contemporary observers may have thought. Traditional customs and patterns of family behavior (which were themselves in process of change) were experienced simultaneously as sources of aid and support and as restrictions on the personal choices and freedoms of young adult women. In this context, the employment of working-class women in factories and stores represented a decisive collective experience. Employment for pay outside the home both fostered a sense of personal independence and value and made possible the emergence of a group consciousness and identification. The latter development was all the more significant in light of women's subordinate position in the labor market, their continued dependence on patriarchal family relationships and, especially, their limited tenure of jobs (for most women) in the years prior to marriage.

In analyzing the changing relationships among pre-industrial family patterns, industrial employment, and social consciousness, *Give us Bread but Give us Roses* steers clear of certain narrow historical formulations which have enjoyed wide influence. The latter approaches have, in various ways, reduced the social factors determining working-class women's response to industrialization to a single dimension of what were multifaceted relationships. One such interpretation of working-class behavior in its encounter with industrial capitalism locates sources of radicalism or social cohesion exclusively within pre-industrial immigrant culture and community life (exemplified by the writings of Herbert Gutman on working-class culture, and those of Virginia Yans-McLaughlin on working-class women and family patterns).[7] This approach neglects entirely the socializing function of employment outside the home for the emergence of a distinct sense of identity and ability to act together among women of the working class.

A contrary interpretation treats efficient capitalist work settings as the catalyst of female emancipation from traditional forms of subjugation. In this view, industrialization promoted a positive individualism, the ideal of economic independence, and the assimilation of modern work habits on the part of young working-class women. (This position is advanced by historians of modernization in women's work and social roles.[8]) This perspective slights the continued impact of class barriers, exploitative workplace relationships and family traditionalism among working women, as well as the problem of collective reaction to these conditions.

In contrast to these two polarized conceptions, the present study places the relationships between women's changing position in industry and older class and family cultures at the center of its analysis. It attempts to specify the domains of conflict and accommodation between these social forces, without falsely idealizing the consequences for women of either modern economic individualism in the form of early twentieth-century employment conditions or precapitalist communal (and patriarchal) traditions. From this vantage point, it can more adequately assess the ways in which qualitatively new social experiences (stemming from women's increased employment) transformed working-class women's sense of their needs and social position, and their ability collectively to express this consciousness.

In tracking down such collective expressions, *Give us Bread but Give us Roses* relies not only on the reports of external observers (journalists, social workers or government investigators), but also on the documents produced directly or indirectly by the activities of working-class women. The diverse group that left fragmentary records of some kind had a wide range of public or organizational involvements. It included anonymous women who participated in discussions in working girls' clubs or wrote letters to the labor press, speakers at strike rallies, committed trade union members whose correspondence has survived, and women who became full-time organizers for the Women's Trade Union League or garment unions. Such working-class women were, in varying degrees, atypical in their organizational connections and also their personal lives, first, with respect to the important minority of working women who were drawn momentarily toward movements for change, and second, even more clearly, in relation to the great majority of working women outside this realm. None the less, the implicit rationale for using critically the expressions of 'exceptional' women to illuminate a broader social reality is two-fold. First, the pre-First World War period was marked by sharp change in women's urban and industrial experiences, and an ebb and flow of social movements and organizations, including some (the settlement movement, Young Women's Christian Association, trade unionism, municipal socialism and woman suffrage) which had points of contact with the situation of working women. In this context, to erect rigid boundaries between women who organized (the subject of conventional labor histories) and unaffected, 'representative' working women (the focus of newer social histories) appears especially problematic. In the early years of these movements, the transitions for working women from 'ordinary' situations to sporadic or lasting involvements were often fluid. Common experiences of family migration, poverty, starting work outside the home, and so on, and related cultural attitudes, probably had a salience in working women's consciousness across this spectrum, and may be distilled in more articulate form from the accounts of 'exceptional' women.

Second, on the specific problem of the elaboration of a critical response to their situation, those 'exceptional' women who were engaged in collective organization were, by virtue of this activity, in a privileged position. Analysis of their attitudes and public statements can reveal just how far such a consciousness did develop. The analysis also sheds light on the processes, involving sustained communication with other working-class women, and public action and presentation of ideas, which facilitated this result. It is then possible to specify the factors which enhanced or limited participation in the process of organization by broader sectors of working women.

The dialectical perspective which informs this study is closely tied to the examination and critical use of classical social theories of consciousness. In chapter 3, Sarah Eisenstein assesses the value of Marxist, Mannheimian, neo-Weberian and functionalist insights for the analysis of consciousness formation among subordinate groups, and working-class women in particular. This discussion yields certain key conceptions: the Marxist notion of dynamic structural conditions which generate a socialization of consciousness; Mannheim's concept of the 'self-discovery of the social group' that derives from its confrontation with external definitions of group characteristics; and the notion of a 'negotiated response' on the part of a subordinate class to dominant and radical ideologies.

Critically applying these ideas, *Give us Bread but Give us Roses* develops certain historical arguments which have been mentioned above. Four of these can be summarized briefly.

First, the problems of domestic isolation, the perception of women's roles as 'natural', and other conditions which barred a collective self-awareness were experienced differently by women of different class positions in the nineteenth century. The avenues of participation in religious and moral reform movements, which allowed middle-class women to overcome the isolation of family relationships and (for many) to move toward feminism, were not available to women of the working class. For the latter women, the processes of 'self-discovery' and emergence of a group consciousness depended on employment outside the home, and were spurred and also limited by the character of new employment patterns.

Second, Victorian ideals, and particularly norms concerning women's leisured and purposive activities, had passed their peak of influence and rigorous formulation by the early 1900s. The standards defining accepted occupational pursuits for 'respectable womanhood,' as reflected in popular advice literature, had loosened somewhat. None the less, these standards of behavior and sexual propriety continued to deny working-class women in employment the social recognition of a womanly status. Yet they also provided a central point of reference that affected these women's attitudes toward their own lives and aspirations.

Third, working women's consciousness was not, however, a simple reflection of this dominant ideology. Critical elements surfaced, especially in relation to the exclusiveness and invidious thrust of these ideals. Working-class women's 'negotiation' of social ideology in the context of their own experience led to a redefinition of the meaning of the family ideal, home, marriage, and also female friendships and womanhood, even as they adhered to a notion of the fundamental desirability of marriage as a life goal.

Fourth, the possibilities for working-class women's emergence as an autonomous economic and political force in the 1910s must be judged in relation to the character of this broader consciousness, and underlying social developments. The latter included change in the position of women in industry, their families (especially as this was affected by new patterns of wage-earning), and immigrant communities. Both the great successes of the period, i.e., the unparalleled initiatives and organization of women workers, and its limits, in working women's dependence on upper-class and middle-class women 'allies' in the Women's Trade Union League and male trade unionists and union policies, must be placed in this context. The failures of League policy (described by Nancy Schrom Dye and Robin Miller Jacoby), which hindered the emergence of class-conscious, feminist radicalism among working-class women constituents, were largely a product of these deeper conditions of structural position and consciousness.[9]

The essays collected in *Give us Bread but Give us Roses* were part of a larger work planned by Sarah Eisenstein. This was to have included additional chapters on: the broad characteristics of the female labor force in this period; the attitudes of working women to prevailing ideas of woman's nature and ladylike standards; the role of the idea of sexual respectability in enforcing these standards for working women; the development of elements in working women's consciousness which were critical of these influential ideas about women, and their relationship to the process of organization (in unions, the suffrage movement) and ethnic, occupational and regional differences among working women; and a concluding theoretical analysis of the sources and degree of development of this critical consciousness in the early years of the twentieth century.

The following chapter ('Bread and Roses') was a preliminary sketch for this project. The essays presented in Part II of this collection (chapters 3 through 5) were originally the basis for the first half of the larger study. Though unfinished and presented in rough draft form, these essays none the less suggest the approach to the analysis of working women's consciousness which informed the planned study as a whole. It is hoped that their publication will stimulate others to carry forward the intellectual work and struggle for a fuller understanding of women's lives which Sarah Eisenstein did not live to complete.

Bread and roses: working women's consciousness, 1905–1920*

Sociological theory does not provide an adequate framework for understanding the ways in which working women respond to their situation or develop ideas about it. The theory is inadequate in two ways: first, in the sociological definition of women; and second, in the ways in which it tries to deal with problems of value and consciousness. Most sociological theorizing about women has been functionalist in approach, focusing almost exclusively on woman's role as wife and mother, with a bias toward the persistence and coherence of existing value systems.

Functionalist theory sees the value system or dominant ideas of a society as transcendent and determinant.[1] Men's ideas and expectations are seen primarily as a result of their socialization; even in failure to conform to dominant values, men are defined in their terms as deviant or anomic. The only possible outcome of deviance or discontent is seen as adjustment, or else personal and social breakdown results.

A more fruitful approach views people's consciousness or values as flowing from the historical organization of social activity and their place in it. That is, people in a society are seen as actively involved in creating, maintaining or changing their ideas in the context both of the dominant social ideas and of changes in the socio-economic structure.

In a given historical period, one would expect to find a dominant value system to which most groups and institutions tie

*Reprinted from *The Human Factor*, vol. 10, no. 1 (special issue: the liberation of American women), Fall 1970.

their claims to legitimacy. However, one would also expect that this system would be neither completely coherent nor exclusive. Particularly where some groups or classes are more powerful than others, or where different groups have radically different social experiences, one would expect to find conflicting responses to the dominant values and at least elements of different systems of values. It would also be reasonable to expect that in periods of social or economic change new or different values might develop, possibly tied to attacks on or resistance to elements of the dominant values.

In this framework, I want to concentrate on the ways in which working women experience and understand their situation; specifically, I want to examine ways in which women dealt with their increasing participation in the labor force at the beginning of this century.

The period from the turn of the century to the end of the First World War was a critical one in the development of women's participation in the labor force. Pushed by economic depression in the mid-1890s and in 1903–4[2] and by the disruption of family and other social relationships by urbanization or immigration, and pulled by the need for cheap and unskilled labor in industrial enterprises, women entered the labor force in increasing numbers through the late 1890s and the early years of this century. The extent of increase is indicated by the fact that in 1890 a little over one million women were employed outside the home: twenty years later, in 1910, the figure had risen to about eight million.[3] Later, the war created new openings for females and new pressures to work – patriotic appeals, the absence or loss of the breadwinner, war inflation, etc.

The period from the turn of the century to the outbreak of the war also marked the first major growth of permanent union organization among women workers. There had been attempts at organization among women at least since the 1820s, and women had participated in the Knights of Labor and the early A.F.L. unions, as well as in independent efforts of their own, later in the nineteenth century.[4] Not until shortly after the turn of the century, however, were sufficient numbers of women involved in the labor force with intensity or continuity enough to provide the basis for permanent organization.

In addition, the garment industry, the major employer of urban females and the site of the most extensive, successful organization of women workers, completed a phase of expansion and consolidation. Some of the conditions for workers worsened.[5]

This expansion of union activity is important in defining the period in which to investigate working women's consciousness. Union activity in the first place, indicates significant identification with work, or at least its salience in one's life. Second, women involved in organizational activity are more likely to have occasion to develop and articulate their ideas, and to answer challenges to their position. They are also more likely to leave some record of their consciousness.

This time period was also notable for much activity in women's suffrage and feminist agitation in general. Middle-class women increasingly demanded full political and economic participation. Significant numbers either attempted to pursue professional or organizational careers, or defended their right to do so if they wished. They faced a great deal of ideological and practical resistance.

Although these middle-class women often attempted to join forces with working-class women who did encounter similar opposition, their experiences on the whole were different; this discussion will concentrate on working-class women. While middle- or upper-class women who worked had at least in part ideological reasons for doing so, working-class women often had no choice. How did the working-class woman deal with the conflicts between woman's role and having to work? What impact did this situation have on her expectations and ideas?

A number of elements must be examined to understand the consciousness of working women in this period. First, we need to understand to what degree working women accepted the generally dominant values and orientations toward women – that woman's place was in the home, eventually as wife and mother, that she was retiring, passive, and delicate, the custodian of a fragile morality, etc.[6] Second, we need to have a sense of how women understood what it meant to be a woman working, including if and how they perceived special problems or implications for women in the work situation. Third, we need to see whether women, through dealing with their conflicts and problems, developed new forms or elements of consciousness. For instance, in their trade union activity, perhaps they developed ideas that might be said to represent a particular working women's consciousness.

Method of the investigation

People at the bottom of a social order rarely leave explicit written records of their ideas and perceptions of the world.[7] They have not often had the leisure or the occasion to produce diaries, personal letters, or books. Nor have they generally had control of means of mass communications, such as newspapers and magazines. This study relies, therefore, on records and books produced by others about working women. These documents are of two kinds. First, there are government investigations and hearings about the conditions and problems of women and child labor during the period. These elicited information about hours and wages, violations of safety regulations, etc., and are not especially useful for understanding what workers thought about their situation. Second, the middle-class reform impulse of the period produced large numbers of books and reports about working women, written primarily by women active in various reform organizations: The Consumers' League, the Y.W.C.A., and the National Women's Trade Union League. Some of these reports were summaries of investigations – often earnestly 'scientific,' complete with questionnaire forms and graphs. Some inquiries into working conditions of women in industry included interviews or summaries of interviews with working women.

Another group of these books summarize experiences in working with working women in various organizations or in strikes, and are written primarily by the members of the Women's Trade Union League. A third type consists of accounts written by middle- or upper-class women who took factory or service jobs to find out what they were like. Some of these women had a scientific, relatively investigative approach; others were seeking literary or moral ammunition.

These sources vary in usefulness. The picture of working women and their ideas is filtered through the concerns and preconceptions (sometimes bizarre, often condescending) of the reformers. In addition, the books were usually written with a view to convincing the public of the need for legislation, regulation, and concern, so there is often an emphasis on wages, hours, working conditions, and the pathetic.

There are, also, some records left by working women themselves – autobiographies, letters, and articles. Most of these were produced by unionized women, and often by the most active among these, or by women who were in at least some contact with union or reform organizations. They were certainly not typical or representative of all working women. Most women were not organized at all, to say nothing of involvement in national organizations. However, the majority of unorganized and isolated women workers tended not to have any reason to express themselves publicly on the subject of work, excepting women who were presented by employers as exhibits against protective legislation.[8] Or, if these women did speak out, no one saw fit to record their views for posterity.

Organized women were probably the most likely to be able to react sharply to their situation and to formulate new ideas and orientations. They were not likely, though, to be totally dissimilar in reaction from other women. If their ideas are not strictly typical or representative, they still may be fairly seen as indicative of the direction of development of women's ideas.

Women workers, like the working class in general, can be differentiated in terms of other factors than unionization. The divisions between skilled and unskilled, native and immigrant, worker in factory and worker in shop or office, as well as between the organized and unorganized workers, complicate any analysis of women workers in the United States. Without denying these complications, not only for women but for male workers as well, I want to try to describe the general working woman's consciousness for the period, noting the impact of these divisions wherever they are particularly important.

The development of consciousness

The extent to which working women accepted the dominant value system will be determined by analyzing their responses to attacks on working women rooted in that system, and by evaluating the degree to which they felt that the work situation had special implications or presented special problems to them as women, by looking at their complaints and descriptions of the work situation. By looking both at these complaints and at what women valued about participation in trade unions, I want also to get some sense of what life-styles or goals they considered desirable. Finally, by looking at more general, diffuse expressions, I want to determine how they developed new elements of consciousness out of their experiences.

In 1910, about eight million women were listed as wage-earners by the US census. They were primarily textile mill operatives, garment workers, saleswomen, and domestic employees. Large numbers of women were also employed as laundry workers, waitresses, tobacco workers (especially cigar-makers), boot and shoe makers, printers, pressmen, and book-binders.[9] Although wages varied from industry to industry, they were generally very low, and hours were long and irregular. In the New York garment industry, for instance, women generally worked a 56-hour week, often having to take work home to do after hours as well. Wages for learners, about 25 per cent of the workforce in the industry, were from $3–$4 a week; for average operators, about 60 per cent of the workforce, they ranged from $7 to $12 a week, although sometimes going higher.[10]

Women who worked in department stores in Baltimore averaged around 56 hours a week, with some working as many as 65 hours a week on a regular basis. During the Christmas rush, the average work week was around 70 hours.[11] Eighty-one per cent of the women working in these stores earned less than $6.70 a week, an amount that had been calculated as necessary for a single woman to be self-sustaining.[12]

Working women were usually single and young – the average period spent by women in industry was from age fifteen to twenty-five.[13] Married women who worked were generally forced to by unfortunate circumstances; they were widowed, divorced, or separated from their husbands, or had husbands who were sick, injured, or unwilling to work. A government study in 1908 showed, for example, that of 140 widows and wives employed in the glass industry, 94 were classified as widows, deserted by their husbands, or with permanently disabled husbands; thirteen had husbands who were drunkards or loafers; ten had husbands who were temporarily sick or injured; seventeen were married to unskilled workers with minimal incomes; and only six were married to regularly employed, skilled or semi-skilled, workers.[14]

Nevertheless, working women were the objects of much disapproval and censure. Woman's place was in the home; by venturing outside it, for whatever reason, she risked all sorts of suspicions as to her womanliness and moral character, and was subject to accusations that she was undermining basic social institutions and ideals.

Elizabeth Butler, writing about women employed in department stores for the Russell Sage Foundation in 1908, reported:[15]

> Baltimore is not yet consciously a city of working women. Women work, it is true, in factories, stores, and offices, to a number proportionately as great as in other eastern cities, but Baltimore has never agreed that it is desirable. 'We regret the necessity that compels some women to work,' the traditions of the city seem to declare. 'Properly speaking, the cost of their maintenance should be borne by their families.'

Disapproval tended to make some women, at least, ashamed of working at all, and defensive about their situation.[16]

> The attitude of society toward women . . . has had no inconsiderable influence. Disapproval has so frequently been voiced against the women who sought employment in shop or factory, so much unjust and shallow criticism has been uttered against the woman who has been forced into line with the present economic and industrial organization, that it is not surprising many working girls are sensitive about admitting their occupation.

This was especially true of native-born women in small or medium-sized cities where they were not so likely to be insulated from direct contrasts between their situation and the 'normal' woman's life as were their sisters in the large working-class communities and slums of the major cities:[17]

> There is considerable class feeling in the town, and the expression 'only a factory girl' is frequently heard. Some of the girls are sensitive and shrink from the social ostracism, while others appear to find it quite diverting that their old schoolmates . . . should pass them by as strangers.

Thus, even in a group which might be expected to be among the most susceptible to disapproval rooted in the major values of the period, and which was, in fact, one of the groups least likely to take part in union organization – that is, among native-born girls in small midwestern cities – there was some resistance to censure.

Disapproval of women going to work, and attacks on women for doing so, generally had three basic components or approaches. Women working was seen as inconsistent with maintaining a home and raising children – going to work was viewed as, in some sense, an attack by women on the home and the institution of marriage. Second, it was argued that women did not really need to work, that they did so to earn 'pin-money' or to finance their wardrobes. This was connected with the third argument, that women competed unfairly in the labor market, bringing down wages and lowering conditions in the shop.

The first phase of the attack was probably the most insidious and the least consistent. It accused women of undermining the structure of the family when, in fact, they had usually been forced to work by the inability of the traditional family to support its members. It censured women for attacking the homes which they were usually struggling to maintain and it implied that working women had rejected their traditional roles when they were fighting to reconcile those roles with necessity.

Most working women accepted marriage and motherhood as basic life goals. Even 'Mother' Mary Jones, the intrepid labor organizer who waged the class struggle fiercely into her nineties, thought women should work only if it were economically necessary;[18]

A great responsibility rests upon women – the training of the children. This is her most beautiful task. If men earned money enough, it would not be necessary for women to neglect their homes and their little ones to add to the family's income.

Rose Schneiderman, originally a cap-maker and later president of the New York Women's Trade Union League, did not share this sanguine view of marriage and motherhood, but she reports the importance of marriage to most young working girls:[19]

Frankly speaking, the average working woman . . . is looking forward to getting married and raising a family. Perhaps [professional women] disapprove of such frivolity, but then, these are facts and girls will be girls even though they work for a living.

A union secretary for the cigar-makers found the attitudes of southern white women about marriage to be the major obstacle to union organization among them:[20]

they have been taught to think that marriage is the end and aim of their existence. They not only believe the preaching that 'woman's place is in the home' but they are ashamed to be caught out of it, and they are afraid to join a union of workers for fear it will look like a confession that they may not land a husband and so escape from a factory.

Working women also seem to have agreed that, once married, a woman should not have to work; ideally, marriage marked the end of her period in the factory: 'I'm a lady now. I'm married and don't work;' 'Ain't she lucky! She hadn't been workin' no time hardly before she married.'[21] They thought it was legitimate for married women to work, though, if their husbands were temporarily or permanently unable or unwilling to support them. A laundry worker in New York described her employment: 'The laundry is the place . . . for women with bum husbands, sick, drunk, or lazy.'[22] And a woman working at folding circulars argued that 'A married woman hadn't ought to have to work . . . unless her husband is sick or misfortunate.'[23] A married woman who had to work for her living was an object of pity, and her marriage was seen as unsuccessful or unfortunate.

Even women atypical enough to become union organizers often stopped or curtailed their activities if they married.[24] Active participation in union organization was seen by most women (not only southerners) as dangerous to marriage prospects. Rose Schneiderman writes that her mother opposed her early union activity on those grounds, and adds that her predictions of spinsterhood were accurate.[25] However, if she and the many other women organizers who remained single viewed organizational activity and marriage as exclusive alternatives, none seems to have left any indication that she regretted her choice.

The desirability of marriage was linked, for working-class women, to the undesirability of their jobs in factory or shop. Marriage was often the only way out of the factory. This does not mean that working-class women did not value the activity, social contact, or increased independence which might be associated with taking a job. Despite Mother Jones – 'nor do I believe in "careers" for women, especially a "career" in factory and mill'[26] – there seems to be substantial indication that young women looked forward to working, at first, and enjoyed the sense of competence and importance which accompanied earning one's way. Many also seem to have expected to be able to advance to more skilled or more interesting jobs and higher rates of pay. Narrow opportunities for advancement and the drudgery and oppression of factory work generally killed whatever interest they might have had in pursuing work as a 'career,' and reinforced their commitment to, and dependence on, marriage as a goal.

Clara Lemlich, a young garment worker who had played a dramatic role in initiating the general strike of shirtwaist makers in New York in 1909, described this process at a meeting at Cooper Union in April, 1912:[27]

> In the beginning they are full of hope and courage. Almost all of them think that some day they will be able to get out of the factory and work up, but continuing work under

long hours and miserable conditions they lose their hopes. Their only way to leave the factory is marriage.

Thus to the extent that they were touched by the expectations generated by middle-class women about careers and occupational importance for women, working girls were generally forced to abandon or reject them and (with the exception perhaps of women who developed careers in the unions) to substitute marriage. As Rose Schneiderman argued, it was not possible simply to apply to factory work the approach which middle-class women were developing toward professional careers:[28]

> [the] mistake . . . is in the idea that there is a career in industry or in the department store. Those of us who have worked in the factory or store know that there is only room for one at the top and the rest must struggle along until they get married or die . . . . Frankly speaking, the average working woman does not want a factory career, as there is no such thing.

Some of the more active women had a very acute perception of the ways in which oppressive factory conditions and pressures toward marriage reinforced each other. They rebelled at reasoning which seemed to them to reduce marriage to an escape route. At the same Cooper Union meeting Mollie Schepps, another shirtwaist maker, attacked that reasoning:[29]

> Another reason against woman suffrage is that equal say will enable the women to get equal pay and that equal pay is dangerous. Why? It would keep women from getting married. Well then, if long hours and starvation wages are the only weapons or encouragement men can use to induce marriage, it is a very poor compliment to them, and in the name of a purer marriage we must have equal say as we have found from experience that men cannot get married alone.

If working women were basically committed to marriage and motherhood as goals, they were quick to respond to what they saw as hypocritical use of the symbols of womanhood in attacks on working women. In doing so, they began to develop what was really an analysis or critique of the social or structural assumptions behind these symbols. Melinda Scott of the Hat Trimmers Union replied at the Cooper Union meeting to a speech by a state senator about the glories of motherhood in which he invoked the story of the Roman matron Cornelia who, asked where her jewels were, pointed to her two sons:[30]

> And how then do we find the modern Cornelia? Operating a sewing machine with a child at her breast, working to keep her 'jewels' from starvation and the poorhouse. Sacred motherhood! What a farce! . . . We working women cannot help wondering when we hear all this gush about the home how many of us would have a home if we did not go out to work for it.

Clara Lemlich, in the speech cited earlier, attacks both the 'escape' notion of marriage and the notion that it is possible for women to depend on men for their livelihood:[31]

> the only way to leave the factory is marriage. How do you like such a marriage? A girl is ready to give herself to any man who will make the offer! But I am sorry to say that there are thousands of our working girls who are soon disappointed because right after they are married they have to go back into the factory because their husbands are not making enough money to keep a home.
>
> Men tell us they want to relieve the burdens of women. We have many widows in this great city alone. . . . Just go through any of the public buildings at midnight and you will see old and middle-aged women on their knees scrubbing away the dirt that men of business have brought in during the day. That gives you a picture of how well men carry the burdens of women.

In both speeches the implicit argument is that many aspects of the traditional notions of womanhood and motherhood assume presence of a stable marriage and prosperous household – one or both of which are, because of social and economic conditions, unattainable by most working women.

Something of this argument seems apparent also in working women's comments on the notion of being ladylike and proper. Mother Jones may have evidenced a sharper class analysis

than others when she urged, 'No matter what your fight . . .
don't be ladylike! God almighty made women and the Rocke-
feller gang of thieves made ladies,' but women in the labor
movement generally seem to have sensed that certain standards of propriety helped to maintain docility in the industrial
situation. A woman organizer for the Amalgamated Clothing
Workers complained of southern women: 'They think it is unladylike to join a union . . . lodges and unions are for men, and
women will lose the respect of men if they take part in public
discussions and strikes like men.'[32] Lillian Matthews (who was
not working herself) noted in San Francisco as well that
'aggression on the part of women has received so large a
measure of condemnation and ridicule that women have naturally been hesitant about making vocal any complaints or
demands.'[33]

Again, some women at least seem to have begun to reject
the values implicit in these notions of propriety:[34]

> We want men's admiration but we do not think that it is
> all there is to live for . . . Besides, we cannot play at the
> simple idiot and worship men as heroes, as we are not
> angels, nor are they gods. We are simply in business
> together and as such we refuse to play the silent partner
> any longer.

It is improbable that women like Mollie Schepps or Clara
Lemlich had a well-developed ideological criticism of the major
values of their period with regard to marriage or standards of
female propriety. However, in response to censure of themselves or women like them because they worked for a living,
they began to be aware of the social and economic assumptions
behind the values on which that censure was based.

The second major element in criticisms of women working
was the argument that women did not have to work, that they
could be adequately maintained by their families and were not
financially responsible for any dependants themselves:[35]

> There are still many people who believe that women come
> into industry in a very casual way; that they are not very
> earnest about it; that their chief desire is to obtain

through it extra spending money, and that men are their natural protectors.

The argument had significant currency at least as far back as the Civil War, when it was complained of in connection with the formation of the Working Women's Association.[36] Whatever its descriptive validity then, it had little relevance forty years later. Most women who worked supported themselves completely; many were also responsible for the support of their children (and sometimes their husbands) or contributed to the maintenance of their parents or siblings. For example, after the fire in the Triangle Shirtwaist Company, the Women's Trade Union League published a summary of the budgets of 65 of the victims: fifteen contributed practically all of their salary toward the support of their families; nineteen were the whole or main support of their families; twenty-one sent substantial support to dependants in Europe; and twenty-one were either alone in New York or one of two sisters living together. Most were very young – their average age was nineteen.[37]

It is not surprising, then, that women should attack the idea that it was not necessary for them to work:[38]

The woman who works for pin-money will soon give up the struggle – it is too hard, the hours too long, and the wages too low for her to continue unless she has to.

[As for the argument] that girls spend nearly all their money on dress, it is almost wicked to speak of dress when ... thousands ... sit up at night making their own clothes, and if the girls dress fairly well, why not? ... It is not so much a matter of spending wisely as how to procure a living wage and have some to spend.

They also refused to accept the argument that, since they generally spent fewer years at work than men did, their salary was less important.[39]

Does it cost you less to feed and clothe your daughter than it does your son? Is your daughter so much stronger physically that she is able to work 10–15 hours for small pay where your son works only eight hours ...

The third argument against women working, connected with

the assertion that women didn't really have to work, was that women lowered wages and standards for working men. Many male workers, including those in unions, resented working women and viewed them essentially as so many scabs. There was some basis for their resentment; women were willing to work for lower wages, and often under worse conditions, because they had no expectation of being able to get any that were better. Women were also used, not to compete directly for men's jobs, but often to replace them when mechanization transformed originally skilled jobs into unskilled ones – management used the opportunity to substitute a cheaper and more docile labor supply.

However, it was possible to use female labor in this way in large part because women were unorganized, a situation for which the men's unions had some responsibility. Through resentment and indifference they had failed substantially to support the organization of women workers, and had often excluded women deliberately from their struggles and settlements. For instance, one of the provisions of the first negotiated agreements between the cloak-makers and their employers read 'that no part of this agreement shall apply to females employed by the Cloak Manufacturers Association.'[40]

Union women tended to blame the men in the labor movement for much of the tension between male and female workers, and for the difficulty they often encountered in getting women to organize:

> the men in the shops are to blame for not taking the girls
> into their organization when they first entered the shops
> . . . (they are) making the girls feel . . . that they are
> interlopers. Naturally the girls resent this.[41]

> It is just a year since the girls joined the union. They were
> practically forced into the union by the cutters – and the
> contracts of last year brought no material gain to the
> women workers. Owing to this fact it was difficult to keep
> the union spirit of the girls alive . . .[42]

However, especially during the war, because of employers' attempts to use the influx of women into the labor force to attack union standards, women also developed an appreciation of the ways in which employers manipulated the differences between men and women workers to their advantage:[43]

> those who know say that the women have been hired [as streetcar conductors] not because there is a real shortage of men, or to replace employees who have gone to war, but to punish the men for their strikes in 1916. The women are being used as a threat to keep the men 'well-disciplined' and to prevent the spread of union organization among them.

Women workers, at least those who were organized, seem to have been strongly committed to the principle that they needed to organize together with men, that 'competition among workers is a disastrous thing. . . . The salvation of the working woman does not lie in competing with her fellow worker, but in . . . standing shoulder to shoulder with him.'[44] Although trade union women sometimes argued that for practical or organizational reasons certain groups of women should be organized separately from men,[45] they did not develop a view which placed primary importance on organizing as women rather than as workers.

Women workers did think, however, that there were special problems inherent in the work situation for women. They worried about the impact of long hours on their ability to care for a household, and for their children, if they were married; and they were afraid of the effect of low wages and uncertain employment on their ability to maintain a stable home.[46]

> You cannot call it a home where we [working people] go home at night to rest our weary bones for six or seven hours. We are like the birds of the air with their nests and when a storm comes there is no more nest. . . . When she [a working woman or widow] gets home at night she is too tired, she cannot attend to her children.

They were also concerned about the effects of long hours, strenuous work, prolonged standing, and unsafe conditions on their health, particularly on their ability to bear and raise children. Middle-class women writing about working women were especially concerned on this score, citing much medical evidence (which seems to have been considered respectable at that time)[47] about the harsh effects of prolonged standing on the 'future mothers of the race' and urging one day a month 'sick leave' for women. Working women themselves tended to complain about exhaustion, pain, and irritability, but they seem also to have worried about the long-term effects of the conditions under which they worked.

The aspect of employment which was most distressing to women was the degree to which it exposed them to improper sexual advances or to personal abuse or insult. Although the publicity given to this aspect of employment in factories or stores was probably exaggerated, and stories about actual seduction or channelling into prostitution certainly were,[48] there was enough unpleasantness to cause serious apprehensions among working women.

Concern about the 'immorality' of practices in factories was sometimes so acute as to play a role in a strike. Leonora O'Reilly, one of the best-known women organizers of the period, describes a strike of corset makers in Kalamazoo, Michigan in 1912:[49]

> an unscrupulous management where small wages are paid
> for useful labor in the factory – while the wages of sin it
> offers to the young girls who will 'pay the price' are
> alluring; first, she receives good and easy work while in
> the factory, with all the little attentions which can make
> the hard, dull day of the factory girl more bearable – add
> to this, that for the favored ones there is always a chance
> for a gay time somewhere at night after the day's work.
>   When the strike started the older women thought this
> an opportunity to start a moral as well as a sanitary
> house-cleaning in one shop . . . they believed the whole
> people would rise up to protect them.

Salesgirls and waitresses, because of their contact with customers, were particularly susceptible to uninvited approaches. Women who worked in department stores were said to be especially wary about their relationships with fellow workers, for fear of incurring suspicion.[50] 'I don't make friends in the stores very fast because you can't be sure what anyone is like.'[51]

Waitresses disliked the practice of tipping because of what

they saw as the connection between the personal relationship it implied with a customer and insulting advances:[52]

> girls have to live on tips . . . you have to put up with it or starve. The majority of girls . . . if they could get a good living would be glad to do without tips . . . . Girls in restaurants have greater temptations than most girls. Advances are always made, especially in certain districts. A great number go wrong because of so many advances.

Even where actual incidents were not frequent or serious, the impact of the underlying contempt for working women as women was important, especially in a period for which the official sexual values were still basically Victorian.[53]

The most important sort of dissatisfaction among working women, in terms of understanding what they wanted out of life and work, was generally expressed in relatively vague and diffuse ways. This statement by two cousins who were garment workers in New York is probably one of the most expressive descriptions of working women's lives:[54]

> We only went from bed to work and from work to bed again . . . and sometimes if we sat up a little while at home we were so tired we could not speak to the rest and we hardly knew what we were talking about. And still, though there was nothing for us but bed and machine, we could not earn enough to take care of ourselves through the slack season.

This passage expresses their frustration with a life which made social relationships extremely difficult, and almost destroyed the possibility of an active mental or cultural life.

There is a further indication of this frustration in the emphasis which women placed on certain aspects of participation in union activity. Although they recognized and appreciated the importance of unions in establishing decent wages and working conditions, women tended to stress other factors in describing what was important to them about belonging in a union.

They emphasized, first of all, that participation in the union developed their intellectual abilities and broadened their perception of themselves and the world. Over and over again, women insisted that the most important thing about the union was that it made them think.

> But the best part of the union is that it makes you think!
> And we working women have got to do some thinking.
> Long hours, working for barely enough to live on, makes it
> hard to do any thinking. . . . If six million women should
> really think, something would happen.[55]

> It isn't that they [working girls] do not want to think, but
> they are too tired to think and that is the best thing in the
> union, it makes us think. I know the difference it makes to
> girls and that is the reason I believe in the union . . . it
> makes us more interested in life and to be more interested
> is oh, a thousand times better than to be so dead that one
> never sees anything but work all day and not enough
> money to live on. That is terrible, that is like death.[56]

Sometimes the emphasis was more utilitarian: 'A trade union tends to educate the working girl. The girls learn to discuss . . . to conduct meetings . . . to debate . . . [they] begin to feel as though they are waking up . . . .'[57]

Second, the comradeship of the union and the wider networks of friendship to which it introduced women were highly valued by working women.[58] 'Many a poor girl is lonely in a new place to work; but when she joins her trade union the girls are all ready to stand by to be her friends.'[59] The intensity of friendship and comradeship in the unions was frequently the result of going through important industrial struggles together. A special element, noted by almost everyone who commented on women in unions, was the degree to which women who were relatively better off were willing to help their less fortunate sisters. Often, the leaders in a strike were the relatively skilled women, usually among the best paid in the shop.[60]

There is the example of the German girl, who though exceptionally strong and well-suited to piece-work herself, tried to organize the other girls in her shop and was fired twice in one year as a result.[61]

> Yes, I am the forewoman in the laundry and I need not

have gone out. But I could not stand the way the girls were forced to work overtime and the boss always protesting against any increase in pay or decrease in time.[62]

Lillian Matthews, in her description of the Cracker Bakers' Auxiliary in San Francisco, indicates how these aspects were related:[63]

The sacrifice of time and wages which the girls proved themselves willing to make for the sake of bettering conditions for their coworkers . . . still shows itself in a tie of personal friendship among the members of the union . . . a feeling of personal responsibility for its members.

Working women themselves also understood the relationship between their comradeship and friendship for one another and their struggles together for better conditions. An immigrant girl wrote the following letter to the organ of the W.T.U.L.:[64]

I don't know if I can tell you in English, but I will try to tell you why I think the stories of *Life and Labor* do not mean much to the Jewish girls. You see they are all pleasant stories and we Jewish people have suffered too much just to like 'pleasant' stories. We want stories that tell of people who want justice – passionately. You see, with the people in your pleasant stories we have no fellowship.

Although this writer was a recently arrived immigrant and had particular reference to her Jewish background, her letter is representative of the attitude of many women.

Just as women developed out of their experience as workers a sense of the importance of collective organization and struggle, and an appreciation of the value of the fellowship of other women won in those struggles, they also developed out of their particular experience as *women* workers an exceptionally rich understanding of what they wanted to achieve through their struggles. This conception was compounded of a sharp sense of what was shut out of the lives of women workers by the requirements of the factory or store, and a more diffuse perception – to which they usually gained access through union experiences – of how these requirements might be changed to allow their lives fuller development.

The following passage, written for *Life and Labor* by Anna Rudnitsky, another young immigrant worker, illustrates these desires:[65]

> But life means so much, it holds so much, and I have no time for any of it; I just work. Am I not right? In the busy time I work so hard; try to make the machine go faster and faster because then I can earn some money and I need it, and then night comes and I am tired out and I go home and I am too weary for anything but supper and bed. Sometimes union meetings, yes, because I must go. But I have no mind and nothing left in me . . . when the slack time comes I am not so tired, I have more time but I have no money and . . . everything is missed.
>
> Romance needs time. We can think about it, yes, but to live it needs time. Music I love to hear and it makes me happy . . . to study, to go to school, I have no time and I have no money. Then the world is so beautiful . . . why if I work all day and do good work, why is there never a chance to see all these wonders?

This spirit impelled the striking women mill workers in Lawrence to carry banners proclaiming, 'We want Bread and Roses, too,' and it was this spirit that Rose Schneiderman tried to explain when she invoked their slogan in August, 1912:[66]

> What the woman who labors wants is the right to live, not simply exist – the right to life as the rich woman has it, the right to life, and the sun, and music, and art. You have nothing that the humblest worker has not a right to have also. The worker must have bread, but she must have roses, too.

Conclusion

The consciousness of working women in the early part of this century significantly reflected the dominant social values of the period. Working women saw marriage and motherhood and a stable home to supervise as main goals. Young girls generally expected to marry, and though women thought it was legitimate for them to work as long as they were unmarried, married women were expected not to work unless forced to do so by economic necessity. Few working-class women wanted a 'career.' Although young women were often excited about going to work in the beginning, the realities of factory life and the paucity of opportunities to move out of it into more rewarding work were discouraging and ultimately reinforced the dominance of marriage as a goal.

The work situation was seen to have negative consequences in particular ways in which it affected women. Primarily, there was the exposure to insults and 'indecent' conditions which factory or store work often entailed, and secondarily, there was exposure to what was believed at the time to be a special hazard to female health, possibly endangering their ability to bear children.

However, despite the degree to which women accepted the dominant attitudes toward the desirability of women working – or more generally, the dominant ideas about what was an appropriate and desirable life for a woman to lead – working women of the period recognized the necessity to work and fought for the right to do so and under conditions roughly equal to those of men. In the process, they began to develop a rudimentary critique of the social and structural assumptions underlying the socially desired female life pattern. They also developed an appreciation of the value of friendship and association with other women in collective efforts.

Finally, working women rejected the view that they were relinquishing their claims to womanly interests or desires by working. Knowing that they had to work, and affirming their right to do so, they also claimed their right to a more fully human existence than the sad routine traced out by many working girls from 'Machine to bed.'

PART II

Essays in the study of working women's consciousness

3

The study of working women's consciousness

Our study is concerned with the consciousness of working women in the United States at the turn of the century and the ways in which they understood their experience as workers and their social position as women in a period of major industrial change. It explores in particular the ways working women understood their situation in terms of their acceptance and criticism of elements of the dominant ideology of the period about women. It attempts to explain their ideas in terms of their exposure to this ideology, on the one hand, and to beliefs critical of it, on the other; the latter category includes ideas current in the labor and feminist movements of the period. Our major focus is to trace the influence of various elements in the situation of working women on their responses to these exposures. This involves looking not only at the availability of various sets of beliefs in terms of their general currency, but also at the channels of community tradition, institutional influence and organizational experience through which working-class women encountered them.

Theoretical perspectives

A number of relevant theoretical issues emerge from classical sociological discussion of the relationship between social structure and group consciousness. While this discussion is not, with occasional exceptions, directly articulated with the situation of women in society, many of the general concepts it develops can be used to illuminate relevant questions. In particular, classical theory suggests the importance of locating the social mechanisms or situations which mediate the influence of social structure and historical change on the experience and understanding of particular groups. This is the question of 'transparency' for Weber,[1] and of 'specifying the channels through which changes in the objective economic structure effect spiritual and cultural changes,' for Mannheim.[2] The historian Eric Hobsbawm, in a discussion of Marxist theory, characterizes it as the question of the 'links between what people actually experience as economy, polity or society, and what actually constitutes the wider economic, political, etc., framework within which they operate.'[3]

The first issue with which we are concerned is the question of the conditions which make possible a primary awareness of belonging to a group of people who stand in similar relation to important elements of social structure, what Mannheim called the 'self-discovery of social groups.'[4] We will argue that the traditional position of women involved particular barriers to such self-discovery on their part, and that participation in the public labor force played an important role in transcending these barriers in the experience of working-class women.

Classical discussion of this question emerged originally from debates on the nature and origin of class consciousness. They tend to deal with the problem of 'transparency' by arguing that the same developments which give rise, on the one hand, to a shared social position, i.e., that of class, at the same time produce the mediating conditions which encourage recognition of that position. Thus, Marx argues that the same conditions which produce the propertyless proletarian in structural terms create the possibilities of his identification with others in the same situation through the spatial concentration of workers in the factory workplace, urban surroundings, etc.; the ease of communication which this creates; and the subordination of the industrial workforce to oppressive conditions which necessitates collective organization among workers. In developing his analysis of the conditions of class formation, Marx emphasizes the role of active conflict as the key element which transforms mere commonness of situation into a basis for collective awareness.[5] Michels describes in almost cinematic terms the ways in which the development of industry and urbanization create a 'spiritually compact mass' among workers, out of which develops a sense of collective 'belonging together.'[6] He emphasizes the psychological impact of social isolation and of military regimentation in the factory and barracks-like housing. Underlying both his and Marx's discussions of the industrial working class is the notion that workers were drawn into a web of social milieux – workplace, urban community, etc. – which came to dominate society and which determined the workers' most important experiences in relation to large-scale, highly organized institutional spheres. This enables them, on a theoretical level, to connect the sociological factors which generate workers' consciousness with the structural developments to which they trace their analytical description of the workers' social position.

This question of collective identification, however, is a particularly problematic issue in examining the development of consciousness among women. The institutional relationships which define the common role of women in industrial society – i.e., those which characterized the development of the nuclear family in the context of industrialization and urbanization – tend to militate against recognition by women of their shared situation. They are not, through their roles in the family, involved in interactions with other women which would tend to encourage recognition of a common position as women in social terms. Rather, those roles structure a situation which is privatized and personal, and which tends to generate a conception of the category 'woman' in moral, biological or 'natural,' rather than social, terms. This is not to argue that women's position in the family is in some sense outside society. Their roles in the family are tied to important social functions; they are affected by and involved in historical changes as these touch the family. But in these family roles women are not historical actors in the sense of participation in the arena of social development where social relations 'are either consciously maintained ... or changed to a greater or lesser extent by conscious human action.'[7]

Explanations of the development of consciousness or political activity among women, therefore, have to deal with the issue of how it becomes possible for them to interact with one another in ways which permit the recognition of common elements in their situations. They have to trace the institutional bases for the socialization of women's experience as a preliminary to discussion of the development of the various forms which such consciousness may take. This is illustrated by discussions of the origin of the American feminist movement in the first half of the nineteenth century. That development has been analyzed on a number of levels: in terms of the contrast between the democratic ideology of American political culture and the disabilities women suffered in law, politics, family relations and education; in terms of women's reaction to a relatively recent narrowing of their social roles and the delineation of a separate 'sphere' for women in the home; as a consequence of the growing affluence of the middle class and the industrialization of some of women's traditional responsibilities in the home; as a response to the ideological insistence of the Victorians on the special nature of women; and as one response to a relative loss of status among older sectors of the American middle class.[8] None of these approaches, however, claims a simple relation between the historical developments it emphasizes and the situations through which women confronted them experientially. Almost all historians of the women's movement see the isolation and privacy of the role of middle-class women in families in the nineteenth century as a situation which had to be overcome in order for collective identification and activity to emerge.

In this connection, most historians emphasize the crucial role played by the experience of middle-class women in the religious revival, temperance, and abolition movements of the period. Participation in these movements may be seen as a natural development out of the background of the early feminists. Alice Rossi has carefully demonstrated the connection between active religious participation and concern with moral issues and the traditionally based upper middle class out of which, she argues, most early feminist leaders emerged.[9] The universalistic content of that tradition made its claims on women as well as men; it is possible to argue that its pull on women was even stronger given the emphasis placed on purity, religiosity, and concern for others by Victorian notions of womanhood.[10] Yet once women were involved in these movements, they met resistance to their attempts to participate fully in the work. Encountering the definitions developed by others can be a powerful stimulus to the development of more authentic definitions by a group itself. As Mannheim wrote in another context:[11]

> Each of these groups sought to redefine its place in society, but in this endeavour it was not only forced to take stock of itself but also to deal critically with a set of ready interpretations. Women used to accept the male definition of their role; more than that, women used to see themselves as men saw them. The awareness of this fact marked the beginning of feminine group consciousness.

It is generally recognized that the resistance of their male counterparts to women's full participation in the reform work to which their conscience led them was an important factor in the intellectual formulation of women's views of their position in society.

More significant, though, are the ways in which women's participation in these movements created the conditions for the experience of collective action and identification with other women. The influence of these early contacts on their awareness of the 'woman problem' and the recognition which they generated of common disabilities are clearly cited by early feminists.[12] And it was out of these reform activities that the concrete personal networks emerged which were so central to the development of the organized women's movement.[13]

The participation of middle-class women in the reform movements of the 1830s and 1840s was therefore an important factor in socializing the experience of those women and laying the basis for the feminist movement. Working-class women at the turn of the century, however, faced a very different range of experiences and possibilities. Participation in voluntary associations was not usual for women of their milieu; nor did they have the opportunity to choose participation in activity outside their families, since they typically did not benefit from developments in household and consumer economics even to the extent middle-class women did. They were not pulled into social activity through an extension of their traditional family roles. Rather, it appears that the creation of conditions in which it was possible for them to identify with one another as co-occupants of a social situation depended to a large extent on their entering the labor force.

The study will argue that for women from working-class families in this period, work in factory or store was their first collective experience in a situation where the social position they shared as women could emerge. This is not to imply that working-class women were isolated from each other as long as they remained in family roles. On the contrary, most descriptions of traditional working-class communities emphasize the degree to which their social networks are sex-segregated, the connections among women within and across generations, and their importance as sources of support, community integration, and the continuity of tradition.[14] But these networks are primarily extensions of family relationships and thus part of a context which people are used to seeing as personal and natural. The identification of working-class women with one another in the context of those relations was a major source of support in daily life. It often served, when women did go to work, as a source of reinforcement of work-based solidarity. But the experience in itself did not provide the basis for identification with other women as members of a social group.

In a certain sense this argument is analogous with that made by Hobsbawm in discussing the potential for consciousness and political action among pre-industrial groups. He argues that peasants lack the experience of structured interaction which might be a basis for perceiving their common situation in social terms. The peasant, he says, sees his situation either as 'natural' and fixed or as special and individual – the focus of his understanding is either 'the parish pump or the universe. There is nothing in between.'[15] This image is relevant to the situation of working women in two ways: it is directly descriptive of their experience, since many of those who went to work in this period were immigrants from peasant backgrounds; and on a more suggestive level it points to the ways in which the move from home to work by women involves some of the same transformations of experience which characterized the industrial working class in general. E. P. Thompson, for example, makes the point that the rhythms of women's work in the home are largely pre-industrial even today, more tied to the content of the task itself, and attuned to a natural sense of time.[16]

Mannheim draws a slightly different parallel between the experience of women entering the labor force and that of peasants and artisans in the formation of an industrial working class.[17]

> It has often been pointed out that journeymen could not acquire a class awareness of their own . . . so long as they lived with their master's family. This common primary group situation . . . blocked the rise of the [proletariat's] self-centred conception of society. The evolution of feminine group consciousness shows distinct analogies. It began at the very moment when women entered vocations. . . . This marked the beginning of the conflict between the traditional and patriarchal interpretations of the feminine role and the views which working women formed of themselves.

The point here is not that women's position in the family is, in an analytic sense, a vestige or holdover from pre-industrial periods.[18] Rather, the argument is that their experience of that position and the quality of their personal relationships are in certain aspects parallel to those often considered characteristic of pre-industrial situations. This makes the development of collective identification particularly problematic for women. For working-class women at the turn of the century, work outside the home was probably a necessary condition for overcoming the consequences of that situation and laying the basis for their 'self-discovery' as a social group.

The second major theoretical issue with which the study is concerned is the relationship of dominant ideologies and value systems to the consciousness of subordinate social groups. Discussion of the consciousness of social groups has tended to move back and forth between emphases on the social-structural sources of people's attitudes, ideas, or value systems on the one hand, and cultural or ideational sources on the other. One major focus of this debate has been the question of the degree to which a given society is integrated in terms of a dominant set of values or world view which shapes the consciousness of groups at all levels of the social system. A value system or social ideology can be 'dominant' in two senses: in the sense that it represents the experience, perceptions, or interpretations of those groups which control the major institutions of the society (Marx's 'ideas of the ruling class'); and in the sense of its effective generalization and influence over the values and social perceptions of people in various subordinate situations. It is over the latter sense of the term that the most relevant discussion occurs.

On the one hand, Parsons may be taken as representative, if in the extreme, of the view that societies are characterized by highly generalized and unitary value systems, adherence to or acceptance of which is the very basis of social integration and cohesion.[19] The paramount value system is in turn specified at various levels of generality through the norms and roles appropriate to members of different sub-collectivities. The norms which are appropriate to actors in different functional subsystems vary in their prescriptions. In this, however, they represent not contrasts to the general value system, but specifications of it with regard to particular functions and situations. While there may be various strains in the system, they represent a lack of integration within it, not evidence of different systems of general value orientation.[20]

On the other hand, there is a tradition which analyzes the values and social views of subordinate groups as separate from and often clearly oppositional to, that of the dominant classes in society. Marx represents one approach within this tradition; Mannheim, another, with his emphasis on the generation of particular world views out of varying social situations and their competition for dominion and allegiance.[21] On a more descriptive level there is Miller's work on 'lower class culture' as a distinctive and quasi-autonomous milieu; Hyman's and Gans's specifications of the values which characterize different classes; Halbwachs's attempt to specify Durkheim's collective conscience at the level of social classes.[22] E. P. Thompson represents the historical version of this argument, with his conclusion that in the period following the repression of British Jacobinism 'there was a profound alienation between classes in Britain, and working people were thrust into a state of *apartheid* whose effects . . . can be felt to this day.'[23]

Both approaches encounter theoretical difficulties. On the

one hand, it is hard to reconcile the Parsonian view with the elementary sociological notion that people's perception of the world is affected by their experience of it. Discussion of the integration of norms with general values in terms of the functional requisites of a system does not deal with the vast experiential differences which characterize different positions in the social system.[24]

Nor does this view deal with the element of domination in the generalization of a set of values throughout society. Systems of ideas do not simply 'prevail' in societies, nor, in situations of social change, automatically develop to reflect new realities. Rather, they seem to be generated in the first place through the attempts of specific groups to establish themselves socially.[25] This consideration is important in the generalization of values as well as in their generation. As Frank Parkin points out, values are rarely generalized upwards, because the prevalence and importance of ideas and moral assumptions in society depend on the degree to which they are transmitted and supported through the institutional structure. The establishment of one set of values as dominant in society, he argues, is best seen as representing the 'socialization of one class by another' which is more institutionally powerful.[26]

On the other hand, approaches which emphasize the distinctiveness or autonomy of subcultures do not deal adequately with the question of legitimacy. There must be some level on which, to the degree that a society is not based on sheer terror or the direct application of force, people throughout a society are susceptible to the claims of a unitary system of legitimating ideas. This may operate on the level of explicitly shared values. It can also operate on the level of an accepted set of 'descriptions of the world' or definitions of what is socially possible.[27] In either case, there must be some basis, on the level of ideas or meanings, for social cohesion. Approaches which insist on the independence of subcultures from the general value system cannot deal with this level of cohesiveness.

Frank Parkin suggests a way of avoiding these difficulties in some of the formulations he generates in his discussion of working-class culture and views of class in England. He argues that it is useful to see the working class's relation to the dominant ideas of the society not as a process of either simple acceptance, on the one hand, or rejection on the other, but rather as a process of 'negotiation:'[28]

> dominant values are not so much rejected or opposed as modified by the subordinate class as a result of their social circumstances and restricted opportunities. Members of the underclass are continually exposed to the influence of dominant values by way of the educational system, newspapers, radio and television, and the like. . . .
> However, since such values are the representation of the interests and opportunities of more privileged groups, their 'appropriateness' as far as the less privileged are concerned is problematic. The tendency among the underprivileged is not to reject these values, and thus create an entirely different normative system, but to negotiate or modify them in the light of their own existential conditions.

His position is that in the English case the working class refracts the dominant view of class and class structure through the prism of its own community experience, practical needs, and patterns of interaction, to produce a characteristic working-class culture which is neither a direct reflection of the dominant model nor independent of it. It is not so much Parkin's characterization of this subordinate culture as 'accommodative' with which we are concerned here, as with the way in which he conceptualizes the process through which it is generated: 'It is from this tension between an abstract moral order and the situational constraints of low status that the subordinate value system emerges.'[29] The formulation is a useful one for guiding discussion of the relationship between dominant ideologies and the consciousness of subordinate groups. However, it is incomplete without some consideration of the effect of other available value systems on the development of consciousness, particularly those which are formulated in opposition to or criticism of the prevailing system. Here Parkin is less useful. He is concerned to argue that the working-class experience cannot alone generate radical consciousness or a critique of dominant values, but that radical ideas must be brought to it through the agency of a socialist party or movement. This leads him to ignore the ways in which the experience, traditions, communal solidarity of the working class may structure its response to radical ideology. In this he is curiously inconsistent – the working-class community is to some extent an active agent, assessing and transforming elements of an available value system when that system is the dominant one, but a sociological *tabula rasa* in regard to idea-systems put to it by the radical party.[30]

It seems more useful to adopt a more symmetrical approach which would examine 'available' ideologies, both dominant and critical, and the elements of experience, relationship, and tradition in working-class life which structure a 'negotiated' response to each. In this form, it will be helpful for organizing our discussion of the development of working women's consciousness. We will find that working women in the period under discussion generally accepted the central elements of the prevailing image of womanhood, but that they did so in terms which demonstrate the mediation of their own experience. Where they developed ideas which were explicitly critical of prevailing ideology, these did not represent a simple reflection of the arguments of the labor, feminist, or socialist movements with which they were in contact, but a characteristic 'negotiation' of them in the light of working women's particular situation.

Research problem

Our study focuses on the experience of women workers in the United States roughly from 1890 to the beginning of the First World War. The women who entered the labor force in increasingly large numbers at that time were predominantly of working-class background. They entered, in the majority of cases, occupations in industry and in the lower ranks of the newly developing white-collar fields.

This was not the first era in which women had gone to work in sufficient numbers to have an impact on popular consciousness. But the extent of the influx was of a qualitatively different order than had previously been the case. Furthermore, this influx took place in the context of extensive changes in certain elements of social structure which impinged on women's situation.

First, changes in the structure of the workforce together with shifts in family relations resulted in changed patterns of participation by women in the labor force. While most women who worked had done so, since the Civil War, because of unfortunate and unforeseen individual circumstances – widowhood, desertion, invalid husbands, or spinsterhood – during this period there developed a body of women workers who were mostly young and unmarried, and who expected as a matter of course to work for a time in their lives.[31]

Second, the wave of immigration in this period had important consequences for working women. Many were themselves immigrants or the daughters of immigrants, and their experience of changes in family structure and work life was intimately connected to the immigrant experience; in addition, the influx of immigrant labor affected the stratification of women's work and therefore the experience also of native-born American working women.

Third, the period was marked by a degree of change in various legal and social restrictions on women in general; although these had a greater impact on middle and upper-class women, they affected working women's situation to some degree as well.

Thus, the personal experiences of individual women who went to work in this period were co-extensive with developing social and economic changes. This allows us to examine the ways in which women understood their experience of work not only on the level of individual women leaving their homes and accustomed networks of social relationships for paid labor but also on the level of large numbers of women doing so in the context of a significant restructuring of women's role in society. However, it is important not to overstate the extent of these shifts. Work still represented (as it has continued to do until fairly recently) an impermanent phase in women's lives; their participation in the labor force was secondary to, and indeed structured by, the expectation of marriage and motherhood. Thus, we cannot treat women who worked simply as members of the industrial labor force who happened to be female, but must examine the ways in which their work experience was characteristically shaped by the primacy of their family roles.

In addition, the period offers an opportunity to investigate the interaction between a clearly defined ideology and the actual experience of working women. The prevailing ideas were rooted in still potent Victorian notions about women's place and woman's nature. Although these had undergone some modification by the turn of the century, particularly as they affected upper-class women, they retained a great deal of prescriptive force with regard to the situation of women workers.

Their basic themes were the assumption that woman's place was in the home as wife and mother, and the image of the lady as the model for all women. The codification of these ideas in what Barbara Welter calls the 'cult of True Womanhood' was at its height in mid-century; even then, however, it was neither internally consistent nor capable of encompassing the complex realities of women's lives.[32] It is, therefore, important not to overestimate the solidity or history of its dominance. In addition, various social developments had, by our period, begun to aggravate the inconsistencies of its prescriptions.

Women were attending college in increasing numbers, and entering the labor force in the professions as well as at wage labor, and there was increasing popular awareness of this. Upper-class women were increasingly involved outside their homes, whether in pursuing conspicuous leisure activities or in philanthropic work which took them into a wider range of social situations. There was consequently some relaxation of the social ritual and standards of propriety enjoined on respectable women. A greater range of social experience was admitted to be consistent with respectability and true womanliness, although the greatest impact of this shift was restricted to relatively privileged women. There was also an increased awareness of the fact that large numbers of women worked outside their homes, and even recognition that many of these did so out of necessity.[33]

Despite these changes, however, basic elements of Victorian ideology persisted in contemporary attitudes toward women. The image of acceptable womanhood remained one which excluded the experience of the majority of working-class women of the period. Despite increased awareness that women were entering the labor force, contemporary opinion still saw that development as basically incompatible with, and inimical to, women's definitive social roles as wife and mother. In addition, work outside one's own home represented the kind of experience which the image of the lady was least capable of incorporating. The conditions of working women's lives, their appearance, the forms of their social intercourse, the character of their relations with men, all undermined their claim to ladylike respectability and to femininity itself. The ideology of the period was, therefore, essentially inadequate to the experience of women workers, both in so far as it condemned their activity as wage earners in value terms and through the narrow range of the descriptive possibilities it allowed in analyzing women's nature.

In examining the relationship between this ideology and the consciousness of women workers, the study will focus on the experience of women from working-class families who worked for wages outside their own home, primarily in factory and sales situations. There are a number of reasons for this choice, and for the exclusions which follow from it.

The vast majority of women who entered the labor force during this period did so in industrial occupations, and although the entry of smaller numbers of women into professional work and the emerging white-collar occupations tended to capture the popular imagination, it was industrial work which was the more representative experience of employed women. Although significant numbers of middle-class women entered professional careers, their decision to work was most often a matter of choice. That decision often reflected an initial awareness of the ideological conflicts involved and even some eagerness to confront them. Women from working-class families who worked did so primarily because they found it necessary in order to support themselves and/or their families.[34] In addition, the conditions under which they worked tended to be most obviously contradictory to established notions of what was appropriate for women.

Women who worked in the relatively new office-based occupations as secretaries, clerks, and typists have been the focus of some interesting research.[35] They represented an intermediate group, in terms both of their sociological characteristics and the conditions of their recruitment into the workforce. To some extent, working reflected more financial necessity than it did among professional women. None the less, the level of education necessary to office work, the degree of career planning increasingly associated with that education, as well as the social/ethnic characteristics demanded by employers, tended to set office workers apart from most other employed women. They are not, therefore, a focus of our research, although certain aspects of their experience will be drawn on for comparative purposes.

Nor is the study concerned primarily with the experience either of domestic servants or of women engaged in manufacture at home, although each situation raises important issues in the analysis of women's work. Some of the growing body of research on women's work, in Europe as well as America, has in fact focused on these aspects, with a stimulating but perhaps misleading emphasis on the persistence of traditional elements in women's work experience during the development of an industrial economy.[36] In contrast, a central theme of this work is the analysis of women's response to the conflicts engendered by the break with traditional expectations which characterized working outside the home. While we make reference to the role which the continued existence of these earning possibilities in the traditional framework of domestic employment played in conditioning the experience of employed women, they are not a major focus of research.

The analytic concerns of the study, then, lead us to concentrate on the experience of women who sought employment outside their homes, primarily in industrial jobs, and primarily because of economic necessity.[37] The structure of industrial development in the period and the patterns of labor force participation among women, further delineate the group with which we are concerned. Working women tended to be overwhelmingly, although not exclusively, young and unmarried. They tended to work for a relatively brief portion of their lives. A majority were immigrants or the daughters of immigrants, and they tended to live and work in large or middle-sized industrial cities in the North-east and Mid-west. Each of these factors helped to structure their experience in particular ways, and to influence the manner in which they understood it.

Most women who worked at this time did so in the period between leaving school, at a relatively early age, and marriage. They did not expect to work after marriage, such being the fate only of women unfortunate enough to be widowed, deserted, married to drunkards, etc. Thus working outside the home, however important its immediate impact, was essentially a temporary phase in most women's lives. This was extremely important in structuring the ways in which women negotiated the tension between the fact of their working and the emphasis placed by the ideas of the period on women's commitment to home and family. It also points to the absolute importance of distinguishing the essentially contingent role played by work in the lives of women from its determining force in the experience of working-class men. The episodic nature of most women's work also raises questions about the extent to which it can have affected women's perceptions of themselves over the whole course of their lives. However, it should not be assumed that the impact of working was necessarily impermanent because the experience was transitory. Peter Stearns, for example, has suggested that, for English women in the same period, a similar experience of work before marriage had significant, though diffuse, consequences for working-class women's contentment in marriage – raising expectations as to personal freedom, consumption and social experience which marriage could not continue to satisfy.[38]

The fact that many working women were of immigrant background was also important in structuring their experience of work. It meant that the dislocation and adjustment attendant on that situation were often experienced coextensively with the changes in orientation involved in going to work. For example, the shifts in a working girl's relation to her family was often bound up with the changing patterns of immigrants' relationship to their children. Indeed, going to work was sometimes an important influence, along with school, in the 'Americanization' of immigrant women, particularly the younger among them. It was often in the shop that young immigrant women learned American patterns of speech, dress, amusement, social relationship – and there also, consequently, that certain conflicts with more traditional parents were generated. The fact that many working women belonged to immigrant communities in large industrial centers like New York, Pittsburgh, and Chicago, also meant that they went to work out of a background in which a majority of the women in their age group did likewise. That is, although working women comprised only a relatively small proportion of the female population nationally, many working women, particularly those from immigrant groups, came out of immediate milieux in which as many as 60 per cent of the women in their age group worked and expected to work for a period in their lives. This consideration is of particular importance for our discussion of the degree to which women accepted the prevailing judgment of the period that their position as workers was anomalous and unnatural.

However, not all working women were young, unmarried, or from immigrant backgrounds. While the latter situations were characteristic of the group as a whole, these factors provided important sources of differentiation in the experience of working women. For example, various ethnic groups placed different emphases on various aspects of traditional expectations about women and these affected their participation in work outside the home – Italians tended to circumscribe the activity of women most closely, and until rather late in our period, Italian women were more likely to work at home manufacture than in factories; Scandinavian women tended to prefer the more traditional setting of domestic service to factory or sales work; native-born women seem to have assigned more weight to questions of propriety and respectability in choosing work. In addition to the direct impact of cultural differences, considerations growing out of the differing situations of various groups also affected the work experience of women. The order of arrival of different immigrant groups, their geographic locations, and the intersection of these with the development of particular industries tended to structure the kinds of work which women did – for example, East European Jewish women working in garment trades in New York and Chicago; Poles and other Slavs in Chicago stockyards; Irish women in more skilled trades like bookbinding.

Married women who worked, whether from the necessity of

supporting a family whose traditional breadwinner was gone or incapacitated, as was true in the majority of cases, or from choice, as seems to have been the case in some New England mill towns, did so under different constraints than did unmarried women. Young women who lived alone, with friends, or in institutions like the Working Women's Homes, faced different situations than did girls who lived with their own families. Those who worked in cities with significant populations of working women had different experiences than those who lived in smaller towns where working women were more of an anomaly; women with certain skills and longer experience of employment faced different conditions than those who formed the pool of unskilled, transient labor. These differences must be taken into account not only descriptively, but in assessing their impact on the development of consciousness. Therefore, the study will draw a number of internal comparisons between the attitudes of women in different situations – i.e., women of different ethnic backgrounds; women working under various conditions and in different sectors; women in various family situations, and with varying patterns of relationship to the surrounding community – in order to examine the influence of these factors on women's perception of their situation.

4

Victorian ideology and working women

In order to understand the ways in which women workers interpreted their position, it is necessary first to delineate the dominant ideology about women for this period. In this chapter I want to describe briefly the major themes of Victorian ideology about woman's place, the origins of those ideas in the experience and aspirations of the rising middle class, and their implications for the general image of working-class women. I will then concentrate on a discussion of specific attitudes toward women and work as evidenced in contemporary advice literature.

The ideas with which women had to confront and interpret their increasing involvement in work outside the home at the turn of the century were rooted in basic Victorian notions about woman's place and woman's nature. These ideas had not developed out of the situation of working-class women, nor were they consistent with it, yet they informed the ideology of the period so thoroughly that they dominated prevailing attitudes toward working women, and shaped the terms in which those women interpreted their own experience. The basic themes of this ideology were the assumption that woman's place was in the home as wife and mother, and the image of the lady as the model for all women.[1] Both were developed in some complexity, and with uneasy insistence, in the early nineteenth century, in literature, popular magazines, religious tracts and public debate.

At the core of these ideas, which Barbara Welter characterizes as the 'Cult of True Womanhood,' was the assertion that 'The true woman's place was unquestionably by her own fireside – as daughter, sister, but most of all as wife and mother.'[2] The home was seen as the sphere in which woman accomplished her most fitting work and truest service. It was there that she was expected to minister to the personal and moral needs of her family, as well as seeing to their material and practical wellbeing: to nurse when they were sick; provide diversion when they were unhappy; remind them of religious truth when they were spiritually uncertain. Marriage was[3]

> that sphere for which woman was originally intended, and to which she is so exactly fitted to adorn and bless, as the wife, the mistress of a home, the solace, the aid, and the counsellor of that ONE, for whose sake alone the world is of any consequence to her.

It was in marriage that it became possible for her to achieve her highest destiny, that of mother. Motherhood represented the acme of woman's achievement in terms of social prestige, religious dogma, possibilities for personal fulfillment. 'In becoming a mother, you have reached the climax of your happiness, you have also taken a higher place in the scale of being.'[4] It also represented her one source of power, since it was only in her responsibility for raising and training her children that she might legitimately hope to influence the moral development of society. She had, in her natural sphere, the opportunity to form 'the infant mind as yet untainted by contact with evil, like wax beneath the plastic hand of the mother.'[5] As mother, she was exhorted to 'acquit thyself well in thy humble sphere, for thou mayest affect the world.'[6] The home was the place, then, where women must accomplish their most 'natural' and traditional roles; the sphere in which they might most fruitfully act out the pious, nurturing, 'sensible' elements of their character.

The home was also woman's place because it was there that she was safest. Physical delicacy, relative intellectual weakness, timidity in the face of harsh contacts or conflict, made it necessary for a woman to look to a protector who could defend her from the world and guide her through its more threatening aspects. In her early years, this was her father, in her later ones, most appropriately her husband. But it was clear that no 'true' woman would want – or be able – to leave the refuge and protection which the home of either provided from the larger world.

Finally, remaining in the home was central to the maintenance of a woman's sexual purity and respectability. The early Victorians elevated the importance of sexual purity and innocence in women to such a degree that they approached denying women any sexuality at all.[7]

> I should say that the majority of women (happily for them)
> are not very much troubled with sexual feeling of any
> kind. . . with [a few] sad exceptions, there can be no doubt
> that sexual feeling in the female is in the majority of cases
> in abeyance . . . and even if roused (which in many
> instances it never can be) is very moderate compared with
> that of the male.

Only 'low and vulgar' women had unnaturally vigorous or evident sexual desires; respectable and virtuous women felt little sexual interest and submitted to 'marital duties' only in the hope of motherhood. 'The best mothers, wives, and managers of households, know little or nothing of sexual indulgences. Love of home, children, and domestic duties, are the only passions they feel.'[8] Home and family were the appropriate objects of the only natural passions a virtuous woman might experience or wish to satisfy.

In addition, the home of her father or husband was the guarantor of a woman's virtue. The privacy and retirement of domestic life preserved that innocence of any remotely sexual awareness which was considered the epitome of feminine delicacy and purity before marriage. The protection of male relatives was designed to shield a young girl from unregulated or inappropriate social contacts with strange men; close supervision and elaborate social ritual guaranteed that she had little opportunity to compromise her virtue. The ideal bride was one whose sexual innocence was complete – and obvious to observers. 'Milton's lofty notion of tried virtue rather than blank virtue would have met few responsive chords in the hearts of Victorian men looking for an ideal helpmeet.'[9] The Victorians' concern with the guarantees of virtue seems somewhat contradictory to their assurance that women were innately uninterested in sex. Certainly, the cultivation of innocence as a sign of purity must have been in tension with its ultimate purpose – for marriage would represent, as Welter points out, 'literally, an end to innocence.'[10] Nevertheless, the identification of women's sexual virtue with the limitation of their activities to the home remained a strong one; her home and family were both the guarantee of a woman's purity and the only natural objects of her passionate concern.

These attitudes about home and motherhood as woman's proper sphere were closely bound, for the Victorians, to the idea of the Lady. It was true in America as in England that 'Throughout the Victorian period the perfect lady as an ideal of femininity was tenacious and all-pervasive, in spite of its distance from the objective situations of countless women.'[11] By definition, a lady remained within her home, dependent on her husband or father for support. She did not support herself economically.[12]

> The women of the middle classes were very consistent in
> their attitude toward being paid: 'they would shrink from
> it as an insult.' The image of the lady as a creature of
> leisure, enclosed with a private circle of family and friends
> and completely supported by father or husband, was
> reinforced by the ban on paid employment.

It was an important part of her status that the men of her family could afford to support her financially. But, increasingly, she did not do work in the home either. She might manage the affairs of the household, but ideally the work itself was accomplished by servants. She might intervene where particular skill or delicacy was required, but her real responsibility was to create an attractive and refined atmosphere in the home, not to actually clean or cook herself.

She was expected to fill her time with 'accomplishments' which were evidence both of her economic superfluity and her refined nature. She might engage in dainty embroidery, light music, or painting. She might read, but not too seriously. And she followed very intricate models of behavior and appearance, which indicated her gentility. Through her dress, her surroundings, and the precise regulation of her social interaction, a lady was expected to demonstrate the exquisite nature of her sensibilities, the delicacy of her constitution, and the refinement of her moral perceptions. Concern with appearances was intimately connected with this emphasis on gentility. Although a lady was assumed to be naturally delicate, sensitive, and refined, she was expected to make sure that her circumstances guaranteed it in the eyes of the community. Even Tocqueville, who found the unmarried American woman far freer and more independent than her European counterpart, remarked that she was 'not slow to perceive that she cannot depart for an instant from the established usages of her contemporaries without putting in jeopardy her peace of mind, her honor, nay, even her social existence.'[13]

The prudery which was so characteristic of Americans in this period was an expression of this concern with appearances. The external evidence of virtue became almost as important as its private reality. Women went to extraordinary lengths to demonstrate their modesty, and to exclude any remotely sexual reference from their experience. Clothing had to be properly concealing, conversation guarded, and language discreet; the lady who covered her piano's 'limbs' with little skirts was perhaps excessive, but her action was consistent with the general attitude which found references to 'legs' too excessive for polite conversation.[14] Even where attitudes were less coy, the delicacy and refinement of a lady's behavior and surroundings were an important indication of her purity and sexual innocence.

Clearly, the image of the lady involved internal inconsistencies and obvious disregard of reality in important areas. The importance of sexual innocence as a guarantee of virtue was somewhat difficult to maintain after marriage; the image of the physical delicacy of ladies, incongruous with the extensive strength needed to survive continuous childbearing under prevailing medical conditions. The refinement and display of her accomplishments were especially important in the period before a lady's marriage, when they were considered essential for attracting a husband. Yet they were hardly the competences necessary to keep him happy after marriage. Welter cites a number of articles which make it clear that some commentators saw the emphasis on refinement and delicacy as something less than functional. They warn young girls of the folly of neglecting practical domestic training and skills.[15] A story published in *Godey's Lady's Book* in 1841 makes clear the different expectations held of 'Sweethearts and Wives.'[16] The young bride, after an idyllic courtship, disregards the warning of her wise old aunt and fails to carry out her duties in the maintenance and arrangement of domestic order. She foolishly thinks that affection and attractiveness will suffice, and makes no effort to control or regulate her servants. (There is no question of her doing the work of the household herself, just of knowing how to supervise and arrange the work of servants.) Things go from bad to worse between her and her husband until he is wise enough to show her how painful the domestic inconveniences are to him, and she reforms. She concludes that there is 'a very great difference between a sweetheart and a wife,' but of course 'would sooner be a wife than a sweetheart a thousand times.'[17]

In part, these inconsistencies represented the distance between a set of ideological prescriptions and the complex realities of women's lives. But they also indicate the tension between a newly emergent set of ideas and the persistence of older values and behavior. The 'Cult of True Womanhood,' with its insistence on home as woman's sole and private sphere, and the generalization of the model of the Lady were, after all, quite recent developments. The emphasis with which they were promulgated indicates that they were not yet solidly or exclusively established. It is important not to overestimate either their consistency or the history of their ideological dominance. They were at their height in the 1830s, 1840s, and 1850s, but even then earlier notions of good housewifery and domestic production still suggested contradictory models.

Until almost the end of the eighteenth century in the United States, standards of female behavior and character reflected a much broader and richer variety of social roles. It will be useful to look briefly at their history.

During the Middle Ages and the early stages of capitalist development in England, women had been heavily and centrally involved in economic production.[18] Although their main social roles centered on the home, the household itself was much more integrated into economic activity, whether in agriculture, trade, or craft production. Women played an important part in their families' economic activities, often a skilled or directing one. They were responsible, in the extended households of master craftsmen, for overseeing and training apprentices, and for organizing and performing certain aspects of the work itself. Their involvement was often so extensive that they succeeded to their husbands' places in certain guilds as widows. Agricultural wives often helped in the fields and were responsible for dairy and poultry production, as well as having a central role in small trade and local markets. In addition, women at almost all social levels were expected to be responsible for the internal requirements of the household. This included doing or supervising spinning, weaving, sewing, the maintenance of kitchen gardens, in addition to cooking, cleaning, and looking after children. They were expected not only to process resources provided by the husband, but often to assist in that provision as well, whether through their own productive activity or through small trade. So, although women's social location was in the home, the household was a much broader and more public institution;[19] and their role in productive work was a source of independence and esteem.

It was only with the greater development and elaboration of capitalist organization, which removed much production from the household and replaced the diffuse ties of master and workman with the market relations of free labor, that woman's tie to the home became characteristically narrow and restricting. Her role in production for the general economy necessarily declined as that work was removed from the household. And, as industrialization proceeded, many of her traditional tasks in the internal economy of the household itself were removed to factories.

The American colonists established households which resembled the older model in the importance of women's productivity. The rigors of settlement, the continual expansion of the frontier, and the importance of small agricultural holdings enforced the importance of women's economic contributions. In New England particularly, Puritan origins reinforced the claims of the material situation with a religiously grounded emphasis on the importance of work and the dangers of idleness. These factors were reflected in an image of women which emphasized competence and usefulness and allowed a greater range of occupations and social contacts.[20]

The influence of this image is indicated in the discussion which surrounded the beginnings of industrialization in the United States in the early 1800s. One source of unease about the introduction of cotton machinery was the 'fear that the female part of the population by the disuse of the distaff should become idle.'[21] The early advocates of manufactures found it necessary to defend the new system in terms that emphasized its ability to provide useful employment to women. They assured critics that factories would educate women in habits of honest industry and elevate 'the females belonging to the families of the cultivators of the soil . . . from a state of penury and idleness to competence and industry.'[22] The early industrialists did not, of course, establish factories in order to preserve older traditions of female usefulness. They turned to female labor because it represented the most easily available pool of surplus labor, and one which they could demonstrate was not being withdrawn from agricultural production, still seen as the backbone of the nation.[23] What is interesting, however, is that, in defending their new system, they could still use the earlier images of women's usefulness effectively. Hamilton argued that 'women and children are rendered more useful by manufacturing establishments than they otherwise would be'[24] and other publicists that women were 'kept out of vice simply by being employed.'[25] Even as late as 1824, Matthew Carey argued that young women who worked in cotton mills would 'contract habits of order, regularity and industry, which lay a broad and deep foundation of public and private future usefulness,' although he evidently also found it necessary to deal with unease at this process taking place outside the home:[26]

> They will become eligible partners for life for young men, to whom they will be able to afford substantial aid in the support of families. Thus . . . the inducement to early marriages . . . is greatly increased . . . and immensely important effects produced on the welfare of society.

In the colonial period, the women of the urban middle class, and of the small, independent farmer class, were evaluated in terms of a variety of models – Puritan goodwife and helpmeet, frontier settler, partner/assistant to the urban draftsman or merchant – all roles which put a premium on usefulness, competence, and full social activity. The Lady was a model only for the wives and daughters of the upper classes or aristocracy.

By the end of the eighteenth and the beginning of the nineteenth centuries, however, the Lady had begun to be generalized into a model for all women. Although older notions persisted, and were often the basis of criticism of the newer model, the image of the Lady began to supplant them as a description of woman's proper nature and behavior. The standards of gentility, associated until then with aristocratic women, became confounded with those of propriety and sexual regularity, on the one hand, and femininity itself, on the other, until the image of the lady became coextensive with that of respectable womanhood.[27]

This was not a simple nor a rapid transition, nor is it an easy one to date. Page Smith discusses the influence of English styles and literature on the prosperous colonial middle class in the third quarter of the eighteenth century.[28] He cites the dismay of a young John Quincy Adams returning to New England after three years in France, to find American girls in 1790 'simpering' and 'affected,'[29] only interested in fashion and society. By the end of the eighteenth century, according to Smith, there were numerous examples of public lamentation over the superseding of older, sturdier images of womanhood by newer standards of fashion and elegance. According to some foreign observers, these standards were not confined to the wealthy even before the turn of the century:

> The salary of a workingman must not only provide
> subsistence for his family, but also comfortable furniture
> for his home, tea and coffee for his wife, and a silk dress to
> put on every time she goes out.[30]

> In vain Citizen Livingston, of venerable memory, recalled
> his fair compatriots to their spinning wheels and to
> conservative simplicity of manners and fortune, for he was
> not listened to. . . . The rage for luxury has reached such a
> point that the wife of the laboring man wishes to vie with
> the merchant's wife, and she in turn will not yield to the
> richest woman in Europe.[31]

However, these developments were limited to the larger cities even in the early 1800s. Change was slower and less clear in rural areas. The influence of older traditions, the pressure of conditions on the frontier and in older farming regions where women's work was still central to the household, even resistance to the aristocratic pretensions of the Lady based on republican and anti-English sentiment,[32] all retarded and limited its generalization. Indeed, there was always an undercurrent of criticism of the Lady as a model, even at the height of its influence; the emphasis on pure idleness which characterized the English lady,[33] for example, was never as strong in the United States.

Even so, by the 1830s and 1840s the idea of the Lady had become widely generalized, the prescriptions for her behavior directed at women of all classes, her gentility and delicacy identified with respectability itself. Gerda Lerner argues persuasively in her article, 'The Lady and the Mill Girl,' that by this period,[34]

> The image of 'the lady' was elevated to the accepted ideal of femininity toward which all women would strive. . . .
> The actual lady, was, of course, nothing new on the American scene; she had been present ever since colonial days. What was new in the 1830's was the cult of the lady; her elevation to a status symbol. The advancing prosperity of the early nineteenth century made it possible for middle class women to aspire to the status formerly reserved for upper class women. The 'cult of true womanhood' of the 1830's became a vehicle for such aspirations.

This new significance of the conception of the lady was connected, as Lerner indicates, to the growth of the middle classes and to their attempt to assert a claim to new social status.

In the first place, the social and economic processes which accompanied industrialization in this period created the conditions under which the generalization of the model of the lady and the cult of true womanhood was possible. The rise of industrial manufacturing and the increased complexity of commercial organization tended to enforce the removal of economic activity from the home. At least in urban areas, the household became almost completely separate from the productive activity which supported it. In addition, industrialization and the increasing differentiation of the economy tended to narrow the focus of women's work in the domestic economy itself.[35] Although nowhere near as marked as it would become toward the end of the century, by the 1830s there was a discernible trend toward the industrialization of some of women's traditional household tasks, among them spinning, weaving, and some canning.[36] The development away from the self-sufficient household was most evident in towns and cities, but even the wives of small farmers were affected by the availability of cheap cotton and ready-made men's clothing. Both trends combined to change the meaning of woman's traditional assignment to the home; as it was dissociated from productive activity and its attendant complex of social relations, the household became a narrower and more constricting location.

At the same time as the home became a more limited situation for women, their tie to it was re-emphasized, and its image was inflated and idealized. The home, and woman as its guardian, became the repository of all traditional virtues, the only place where human relationships and feelings were nurtured, a rose-covered retreat and haven. This may have represented, in part, an attempt to reconcile women to their narrowed range of options and relationships.[37] But it also seems to have been connected to the rise of industrial capitalism in a more particular way. Mary Ryan argues that in the 1830s and 1840s the image of the home developed as a counterpoint to and retreat from the competitive pressures and unsettled social relations of the new economic order.[38] The home was the only retreat from these pressures, the place where older values might be preserved, where permanent relationships based on sentiment might be established. It was a highly competitive period, and one in which individual economic position was very unstable; the home represented certainty and tradition. And it became woman's duty to maintain it as a haven.

Welter makes a similar argument:[39]

The nineteenth-century American Man was a busy builder of bridges and railroads, at work long hours in a materialistic society. The religious values of his forebears

were neglected in practice if not in intent, and he
occasionally felt some guilt that he had turned this new
land . . . into one vast countinghouse. But he could salve
his conscience by reflecting that he had left behind a
hostage, not only to fortune, but to all the values which he
held so dear and treated so lightly. Woman, in the cult of
True Womanhood . . . was the hostage in the home.

In maintaining the purity and happiness of her home, a woman
not only served the needs of her own family, but upheld the
moral basis of society.[40]

If anyone, male or female, dared to tamper with the
complex of virtues which made up True Womanhood, he
was damned immediately as an enemy of God, of
civilization, and of the Republic. It was a fearful
obligation, a solemn responsibility which the nineteenth
century American woman had – to uphold the pillars of
the temple with her frail white hand.

The twin cults of Domesticity and True Womanhood combined
to idealize the importance of the home, and woman's seques-
tration in it:[41]

Nature made woman weaker, physically and mentally,
than man, and also better and more refined. Man,
compared with her, is coarse, strong, and aggressive. By
confining themselves to the duties for which nature has
prepared them, respectively, the better they will
harmonize. Let her stay in; let him go out.

Finally, as the middle class grew in wealth and position,
they laid claim to the originally aristocratic standards as in-
dices of their own arrival. The leisure and elegance of his wife
and daughters became the sign of a man's success. By them
he demonstrated his ability to prosper without his women's
labor, and to provide the proper setting and training for
gentility.[42]
An Englishman travelling in the United States in the 1850s
remarked that 'an American's wife is the peg on which he
hangs out his fortune; he dresses her up that men may see his
wealth; she is a walking advertisement of his importance.'[43]

Arthur Calhoun cites numerous examples of similar comments by observers during the 1840s and 1850s, in describing what he calls the 'Reign of Self-Indulgence' during that period.[44] The following one is characteristic:[45]

> It is not avarice that crowds our cities with those who are 'making haste to be rich;' it is the desire to be lifted above the necessity of labor. . . . Many of our females in their ambition to be considered 'ladies' refuse to aid their toiling mothers, lest their fair hands should lose their softness and delicacy, and while using these useless appendages in playing with their ringlets, or touching the piano or guitar, they will . . . boast of their ladylike ignorance of domestic employments.

The process of becoming a lady was not an automatic or a graceful one for most middle-class girls. They were partly aided, though, by the proliferation of academies and seminaries which sprang up in the first half of the nineteenth century to provide detailed instruction in the standards of gentility and the intricacies of ladylike accomplishments. Ladies' magazines, which were a new development in the same period, generalized the lessons for those who could not receive direct instruction, and books of advice on housekeeping, like those of Mrs Beeton and Catharine Beecher, included discussions of manners and attitudes among more practical directions.[46]

Gradually, the earlier plurality of models in terms of which women could shape their images of themselves was replaced with a single emphasis. All women, not just the wives and daughters of the wealthy, were presented with the image of a protected, delicate, elegant, pure and idle creature as a model of 'true' womanhood.

Standards of elegance and 'daintiness' in appearance, of sensibility and delicacy of emotion and temperament, were incorporated into an image of natural femininity. The corollary of this emphasis on what was natural in female character and behavior was a relatively new conception of many activities and attitudes as 'unnatural' or inappropriate for a woman.[47] In addition, the dress, carriage, and social setting deemed appropriate to a lady were identified also as those necessary for sexual propriety.

The particular attitudes and behavior of the lady became generalized and established as the standards which any woman must meet to demonstrate both her essential womanliness and her respectability.

This elevation of the standards and experience of a class very different from their own into general principles for all women had very important consequences for working-class women, and particularly for those who worked outside their homes. In practice, they were excluded from the only socially accepted definitions of respectable womanhood. The conditions of their lives, their appearance, the forms of their social intercourse, the character of their relations with men, undermined their claim to respectability and to femininity itself.

Most important, though, was the fact that they worked.

> Women as workers did not harmonize with the philosophy of the Victorians, their deification of the home. Women ought to marry. There ought to be husbands for them. Women were potential mothers.[48] . . . The worker with her own earnings was . . . an affront against nature and the protective instincts of man.[49]

Working outside the home meant that a woman was unprotected, subject to close social and even physical contact with strange men, and to the orders of men who were not her father or husband. Service work in a store or restaurant left her open to improper advances, and put her in the position of serving the personal needs of men with whom she did not have properly sanctioned relationships. The rough physical nature of factory work was antithetical to notions of female delicacy. The conditions under which working women lived and worked made it difficult for them to achieve the dress, carriage, speech, and manners required for the appearance of gentility.

The treatment of working women in the Victorian novel illustrates how far outside the accepted definitions most of them fell, as Wanda Neff indicates in her discussion of the relative appropriateness of different types of working women as literary heroines.[50]

> The factory girl never attained the popularity of other wage-earning women as a heroine in fiction . . . of all

working women (she was) the most remote from the
experience of both authors and reading public . . . the life
of the mill girl lacked almost all of the romantic elements
beloved by novelists. She was not beautiful. Her hard
labour from childhood had marred any natural
endowments of grace and feminine charm. She was
surrounded by noise and dirt, and could not escape being
dirty herself. Mill girls didn't often marry their employers'
sons, and such intrigues as they had with them would
have sullied the pages of a lady novelist. . . . Other kinds
of working girls, those with cleaner jobs, not so difficult to
comprehend, were more attractive. . . . The factory girl
lacked all the qualifications for the ideal Victorian
heroine.

Dressmakers were a more possible subject – although not the
more depressed sewing-women known as 'slop-workers' who
did the rougher types of work like sewing shirts.[51]

Plying a needle did not disarrange her curls, and long
hours of toil brought a waxen pallor to her cheek and
delicate frailty to her fingers that suited the style of
maiden then. . . . Beautiful but poor, she met temptation
on every hand. . . . Furthermore the dressmaker was
generally a lady, at least in a novel. She could be
represented as toiling bravely with her needle the day
after her husband or father went to bankruptcy. Even if
she were not a lady, the novelist could make her look like
one. . . . Unlike the factory and shop girls, she fitted in
with the traditions of sentiment appropriated by the novel,
and she was consequently a popular and useful heroine.

But the most popular Victorian heroine was the governess.[52]

When it comes to the subject of the sufferings of the
governess, there is no dearth of material. The spirited
writing denied the women in coal-mines or nail and chain
works was given without stint to that ladylike heroine of
delicate sensibilities and infinite capacity for forbearance,
the Victorian governess; for what a coarse working woman
could not feel was torture to her finer clay.

The governess was closest to the lady in origin, training, conditions of life, yet even she was in an equivocal position because she earned her own living. Most working women, who worked in industry or commerce, were much farther from the standard.[53] It is not surprising that the novelist's imagination failed when it came to seeing factory girls as representatives of Victorian womanhood.

The complex of ideas I have been discussing were at their height in the decades preceding the Civil War, and most of the evidence I have cited relates to that period. By the 1880s and 1890s, however, various social changes, including the early victories of the feminists, had begun to weaken its hold and point up its inconsistencies. Women were going to college in increasing numbers, and entering the labor force in the professions as well as at wage labor. Even upper-class women were increasingly involved outside their homes, whether in pursuing very conspicuous consumptions, which would earlier have seemed (at best) unladylike, or in philanthropic work which took them into a wider range of social situations. The image of the lady loosened a bit, and began to include subtypes of a more active character: the college girl, the chum, even the career girl. Some of the more elaborate social rituals were simplified. Contemporaries were so aware of the shift that they dubbed the girl of the period (but not for the last time) 'The New Woman.'[54]

There was also an increased awareness of the numbers of women going to work to support themselves. Shortly after the Civil War, commentators began to complain about the 'New Departure,' as they called the large increase in women working outside the home, brought on in part by the war itself, in part by the industrial use of the recently invented sewing machine.[55]

It became fashionable to say that 'woman as a worker was a product of modern time.' Her entrance into the ranks of wealth-producers and wage-earners was . . . deplored by writers as calculated, by thwarting nature's evident design . . . to rob her of special gifts of grace, beauty, and tenderness. The error of the day, it was argued, lay in the thought that woman should be self-supporting, and she

was implored to stop and consider what homes would
become . . . if 'woman was to take her place beside man in
every field of coarse, rough toil.'

This is not evidence of any change in notions of what women
ought to be, but it is indicative of how early it is possible to
trace awareness of the impact of women's increasing participation in the labor force. This awareness is also clear in the
publication of the first studies of women's employment, and
the earliest guides to occupations for women, including Virginia Penny's *How Women Can Make Money* and *Think and
Act* in the decade following 1860. From that period on, there
is a continuous literature of comment, advice, and alarm,[56]
which, even as it insists on the old definitions of women's
place, demonstrates awareness of their growing inaccuracy.

Despite these strains, however, the basic content of the ideology remained the same. In 1875, the Supreme Court of the
State of Wisconsin ruled that 'The law of nature destines and
qualifies the female sex for the bearing and nurture of the
children of our race and for the custody of the homes of the
world in love and honor.'[57] The assumption that woman's natural place was in the home as wife and mother, and the image,
of the lady's gentility and respectability, albeit somewhat loosened now, as the definition of femininity formed the core of
contemporary ideas about what women should be. They were
the basic notions with which women had to confront their
increasing involvement in work outside the home.

And, as previous discussion indicates, this involvement was
precisely the kind of experience which the image of the lady
was least capable of incorporating. By definition, a lady stayed
within the bounds of her home and family, did not do physical
work, and was insulated from all but the most highly structured social contacts. Women leaving their homes to undertake
their own support contradicted these standards on the most
obvious level.

This contradiction is very clearly reflected in a body of literature of advice to working women which developed around
the turn of the century. Just as women in the early nineteenth
century had been instructed by etiquette manuals on how to
imitate the aristocratic lady, they were later guided through

the complicated adjustment to entering the labor force by a series of books and pamphlets on *Money-Making for Ladies* and *How Women Can Earn*. The earliest of these were Virginia Penny's books in the 1860s; others appeared in the 1880s and, in increasing numbers, through the turn of the century. They offer a useful tool for gauging the persistence of the Victorian ideology of the lady at the turn of the century, and for specifying its implications for working women. Their warnings, encouragements, suggestions, and proscriptions present an important picture of the attempt to reconcile or adapt dominant ideas about women to the changing situation.

The books which I have located span the period which is the focus of this study. The earliest, Ella Rodman Church's *Money-Making for Ladies*,[58] was published in 1882; Ruth Ashmore's *The Business Girl*[59] was issued from 1895–8; *What Women Can Earn*,[60] a collection of articles which originally appeared as a series in the *New York Tribune*, appeared in 1898; and Helen Candee's book, *How Women May Earn a Living*,[61] in 1900. Three later books, *Vocations for Girls*, *Profitable Vocations for Girls*, and *The Girl and the Job*,[62] appeared in 1913, 1916, and 1919, respectively.

The earlier books were mostly written by women who were editors or journalists of some sort, and who drew on their own experience as a model in framing their advice. Ruth Ashmore was an editor of *The Ladies' Home Journal*, which issued her book as part of a pocket library directed at working girls. The contributors to *What Women Can Earn*, though, also include women involved in philanthropy and club work, among them Grace Dodge and Mrs Potter Palmer. The three later books were written by teachers and were for use in high schools; they are self-consciously part of the vocational education movement of the Progressive era, and reflect its emphases.

Most of the books include general advice about behavior and attitudes, as well as descriptions of specific occupations, evaluated according to the particular author's standards of appropriateness or desirability.

It is not clear precisely what their impact was on the women to whom they were addressed, but I think it is probable that the literature had some effect in shaping the terms in which working women thought about their situations. Themes and arguments similar to those advanced in these books appear in all kinds of literature directed at working women and girls. *Far and Near*,[63] the magazine of the Working Girl's Clubs, contained numerous articles which develop the same ideas, for example. It seems likely that most of the books cited here had a large audience; all were relatively small and inexpensive, and most were issued in connection with the popular press or with schools. Still, I have little direct evidence as to their actual impact.

This literature, however, is more important for the degree to which it reflected, and to some extent codified, popular attitudes about women and work. These books are not exhaustive of the literature, nor are they entirely homogeneous in attitude, but certain major similarities emerge throughout the period. It is assumed that women who read these books will be concerned with being ladies, with maintaining that status in the eyes of others. It is also assumed that the necessity of working in itself puts that status in doubt, but that a lady may work at a small number of permissible occupations, and under carefully defined conditions. The elements in work situations which a woman concerned with her status must clearly avoid are manual labor, personal service and deference, publicity, and familiar contact with strange men. Above all, she must be concerned with avoiding any appearance of sexual impropriety. The woman who worked was seen as an individual, who worked temporarily, and because of unforeseen and exceptional circumstances, not as a member of a group who expected to work as part of the normal course of their lives, in response to the foreseeable exigencies of their circumstances. I would like to concentrate first on these major similarities, and then discuss the significance of certain shifts in attitude during the period, particularly between the earliest and the later books.

A major motif of this literature is the attempt to reconcile the experience of work and the world of the lady; to interpret the former so that it was consistent with the standards of the latter. In the process, the advice literature indicates in detail how far outside the canons of acceptability most working-class women were placed.

This is evident in the books' own formulations of to whom

they are addressed and the problems they propose to deal with. They conceive of their audience first of all as *ladies*, gentlewomen who shared a certain background of social position and security and who had always been assured of conventional acceptance and respect. Ella Rodman Church addressed her advice in 1882 to[64]

> Ysolte of the white hands . . . [one] of that numerous class who, while not obliged to enter the ranks of recognized working women, strongly feel the need of increasing a limited income . . . those who are not satisfied with being poor and not fitted for hard work.

Ruth Ashmore assumes that 'the business girls' whom she advises have at least some claim to gentle breeding, coming from 'good,' if not wealthy, families. In fact, she devotes considerable space to the possible errors of young girls from socially prominent families on entering the business world, advising them not to discuss how wealthy their families may once have been: 'a well-bred woman never talks of such things; by her behavior alone she shows what her breeding has been.'[65] Helen Candee's book is addressed explicitly throughout to 'gentlewomen;' and the articles in *What Women Can Earn* assume their readers' concern with being respectable and ladylike.

Closely tied to this perception of who their readers are is the image of why they work. Early in the period, this centers on the notion of women who need to earn money to supplement limited incomes, or to meet temporary or exceptional needs, as in Church's book: 'What then shall Ysolte do? Her case is undoubtedly hard – she is totally destitute of a new silk dress, the means to purchase Christmas presents, and various other comforts . . . of civilized life.'[66] The examples were not usually so frivolous; they included paying for sisters' or – more usually – brothers' educations; purchasing family homes, pulling a family through sickness or lean periods. But the emphasis was on the temporary or supplementary nature of the reason for earning money.

A more important focus was on the need of increasing numbers of women to support themselves or their families. Both the title of Candee's book, *How Women May Earn a Living*, and its dedication 'To All Those Women Who Labor Through Necessity and Not Caprice' reflect a growing concern with this. Since the women in question are ladies, however, the fact of their having to earn a living implies some unfortunate or exceptional circumstance.

> A change in your affairs has come. There are urgent reasons why you should economize. Presently you realize that this is not all – you must actually earn the money with which you are to be economical.[67]

> Become acquainted with a woman worker and you usually find that she has been unfortunate . . . [she has been placed] in altered surroundings . . . forced into the world.[68]

> there is a distinctive and growing colony of women who have been bred to ease, if not to luxury, and [are] suddenly thrown upon their own resources and . . . obliged to put their shoulders to the wheel.[69]

Widows are a popular image, as are daughters whose fathers have died or failed financially; old or ill parents may need support; a lady may find that she does not marry; or a young girl decide that she ought to relieve her family of the burden of her support. Whatever the particular explanation, the image is of a woman who has not expected to have to support herself or others, and who is thrust more or less unexpectedly into the necessity of doing so. There is perhaps some slight awareness that these are increasingly common phenomena, but the image is certainly not of women who know as a matter of course that they will have to work.

This is true as well of the image of the young working girl which comes to dominate this literature after the turn of the century. She is a girl who works in the interval between school and marriage, most often while living at home with her family. Like the older woman, she may work to help the family through a difficult period, or in response to financial reverses, or to make otherwise unavailable comforts possible. She may also work, however, for spending money or for the excitement of larger contacts and experience. Even when she works out of some degree of necessity, though, she is rarely pictured as a

girl who has to support herself entirely. It is most often assumed that she can live at home, and rely on her family for
some degree of support and protection.[70] The image, in
addition, is of a temporary phase, i.e., that of a girl working
until, but not after, she was married. Although later in the
period there is some awareness that girls might not marry,
and thus continue to work, spinsterhood was not something
which was planned for or expected. In its own way, as much
as the failure of the family business, it was an unfortunate
accident.

This literature is very clearly addressed, then, to women
and girls who work, but who are not part of a group who expect
as a matter of course, and because of the normal or permanent
character of their situations, to have to work. The image of
who may work, and under what conditions, yet still be a lady,
is quite consciously exclusive. They are very explicitly *not* 'the
"other girls" . . . the hereditary workers.'[71] They are the 'many
poor, proud ones, who could not bring themselves openly to
join the ranks of sewing-women'[72] – but not the sewing women
in the ranks. They may need to work, but they have not been
raised with that in mind, and they have certain standards to
keep up:[73]

> The amount would be munificent to a shop girl, but the
> ordinary shop girl has not the misfortune of refined tastes,
> nor does she have to dress well, nor meet a thousand
> demands because *noblesse oblige.*

The sense of distance between the lady who may have to work
and the common woman worker is very explicit:[74]

> Not that learning and culture would be amiss even in this
> very practical calling – for if Biddy's mistress had Biddy's
> muscle, she would do the Irish girl's work far better than
> the Irish girl does it herself; 'with brains, sir!' being not
> only an addition, but a manifest improvement to any
> combination.

Though not many books are quite so raw in their attitudes
toward the 'red-visaged denizen of the kitchen' as this, there
is a consistent theme that ladies are not suited to or capable
of rougher work. It is accompanied by a vague and uncomfort-

able awareness of the existence of a group of women who do perform that sort of work, and who have always expected to have to work. But these 'other girls' are not those to whom this literature is addressed, and not among those who may both work and be ladies.

The standards in terms of which this exclusion was framed became clearer when one examines which jobs a lady might take and under what conditions she might work. The range of occupations discussed was rather wide:[75]

> One has only to stand during the early morning hours in the waiting room of a station in a large city and observe the thousands of young working-women who arrive on every incoming train, to be impressed with the fact that much of the work of that great city is in the hands of these competent-looking young girls. . . . Probably the greatest number of these women are clerks and saleswomen in department stores; stenographers, typewriters, and bookkeepers make up a large percentage of the total; teachers, dressmakers, milliners, seamstresses, factory girls, nurses and many others are found in this working-woman's army.

But its emphasis and approval were more directed. There was a definite concentration on the traditional occupations for women, 'the three legitimate occupations for *ladies* in what might be called the Dark Ages of women's work,'[76] teaching, needlework, and housekeeping. Teaching was the most unequivocally acceptable of the three, because of its long tradition and because the conditions under which one worked, and one's relation to the rest of the community were most consistent with being a lady.[77]

> Teaching, in spite of its care and anxiety and wearying, tread-mill round of duties, has always been a popular employment with the educated – principally because it is one of the few means of money-making in which a lady may openly engage without compromising her social standing.

Housekeeping and sewing, though, were also approved, provided they were carried out under proper conditions of dignity and privacy. The most popular advice for a lady faced with earning a living, and equipped primarily with her experience as a housekeeper, was to open a boarding house.[78]

> it seems a great mistake for the . . . young woman with the new education, and some old-fashioned notions of propriety, who is looking about for opportunities for obtaining a comfortable livelihood, to overlook the regenerated trade of keeping boarders.

The advantages of this course were that it enabled women to maintain family homes which might otherwise have had to be given up; to earn a living without leaving the safe and familiar limits of their homes; and even, possibly, to do so *through* continuing to maintain their old standards of gentility, as in this rather fanciful description:[79]

> the six or eight people grouped around the board, arranged as if for a small dinner-party, with nothing visible but the central stand of flowers and the ornamental dessert . . . the lady of the house sitting at the head of her table, handsomely dressed, and free from all anxiety.

Such a boarding house was rare, if it existed at all outside the writer's imagination, but the image was important – that a lady might earn her living and remain a lady by inviting a few genteel, pleasant guests into her home, almost incidentally for a fee. It was quite possible, though, to become declassed through running a boarding house, if it attracted a rough or unsavory clientele. A lady who ventured to maintain a plainer, cheaper house was advised to run it through a deputy, or, if she had to appear in person, to maintain the proper atmosphere of respect and distance from boarders who were not her social equals.[80] Despite the possibility of placing themselves in inappropriate relationships of familiarity with men who were their inferiors, running a boarding house remained one of the most popular suggestions, especially for older women. Books went into minute detail in advising on furnishings, menus, financial arrangements, etc.

Later in the period, and in books directed at younger working girls, the possibility of using women's traditional housekeeping role to earn a living was seen less in terms of keeping a boarding house, and more in terms of jobs in the newly emerging field of 'domestic science.' These included teaching cooking, sewing, and housekeeping in schools, and managing or supervising housekeeping functions in large institutions like hospitals, colleges, and hotels. The emphasis was on occupying a position of responsibility and relative status within the institution; and on the acquisition of respectable educational credentials.

Needlework was the third traditional field of work for ladies; here too, however, one needed to be careful about the conditions in which it was undertaken. 'A deft use of the needle is a particularly lady-like accomplishment; but plain sewing is hard and wearing work, and, since the introduction of sewing machines, it is, when "done by hand" anything but remunerative.'[81] It was acceptable for ladies to do fancy sewing, lace-making, or custom dressmaking and millinery, in which they used finely developed skill and their knowledge of taste and fashion. A particularly successful milliner or dressmaker might open a public shop if it were sufficiently tasteful and exclusive, and particularly if she intended to employ sewing women under her; in general, though, these occupations were approved because they were particularly suited to being carried on at home, or by visiting customers in their own houses. Mass production work, however, was out of the question, since it implied more arduous physical labor, carried on in a public, industrial setting.

Ladies 'naturally shrink from ... severe manual labor'[82] and are, in addition, unfitted for it.[83]

> Heavy work must be done, but there are strong backs to
> do it, and only the daintier duties should be undertaken by
> women of sensitive physique and feeling ... the usual
> work of a laundress (for example) requires the strength
> and endurance of peasants.

It was one thing to do skilled custom work in one's own home, selecting one's own customers from among acquaintances and people of similar background, and another to labor, at the direction of strange men and under their control, in a public place, along with other women whose backgrounds were unknown.

Later in the period it became more acceptable for ladies to do some kinds of manual work. In sections entitled 'Industrial Arts' or 'Industrial Fields' advice books recommended such occupations as bookbinding, designing fabrics for industry, fine engraving, leather work and ceramics and upholstering, as well as millinery and dressmaking.[84] But factory work is discussed only in the latest books, and even there apologetically. It was acceptable for a lady to do manual work only if the character of the work were skilled, the conditions under which it was performed genteel, and no heavy physical effort required. The following passage describes what happens to women ranch owners, but it makes clear to any woman what she risks by working in an occupation which violates these standards.[85]

> In appearance they were as knotted and toil-worn as 'the Man with the Hoe.' Their faces showed exposure to the weather and looked like one of the potatoes grown on their farms. They managed in each case to support themselves and a family of children, but it was at the sacrifice of every refined surrounding and every old association; they had, in fact, been metamorphosed into laboring men.

Hard work and harsh conditions deprived these ladies not only of social position, but of their claims to womanliness – they became not only laborers, but laboring *men*. No wonder then, that these books go into such painstaking detail in advising their readers on suitable occupations and working conditions.

Next in attractiveness to the traditional women's occupations discussed above, and gradually superseding them, were newer occupations in store and office. The publication of advice books in some degree coincided with a period in which these occupations expanded and were opened up to women, and they reflect that circumstance.

The term 'white collar' had not yet been coined, but the image of the stenographer in her clean, neat shirtwaist categorized those occupations as clearly then as the more familiar phrase does now.

Office work was considered the most attractive and ladylike of these occupations. Both typewriting and stenography had the prestige of being somewhat skilled, and of requiring a certain degree of education. The work might be difficult, but it was not physically arduous. More important, although one worked in public, and under male direction, the men one worked with were considered most likely to be proper and courteous, and those in higher positions, at least, gentlemen. There were difficulties in maintaining one's position while working in an office – [86]

> Then, when she has five minutes to herself, or in the time before she begins her work, she forgets that she is born of a race of gentlewomen, and she laughs and jests with one of the clerks, or assists in playing a joke on the office boy. After this, has she any right to be offended if the clerk with whom she has been so 'chummy' . . . addresses her by her first name?

– but they were largely a question of remembering one's own dignity and standards in a world with less rigorous ones. The conditions under which she worked, and, for the most part, her employers and co-workers, made it possible for a lady to maintain her appearance, manner and position, if she was careful of her dignity.

This was generally considered to be true of work in department stores as well, although there were more reservations. The most desirable jobs of this sort were the more senior and supervisory positions:[87]

> The cash girl is not an object of envy, lagging about the store dressed like a child from an orphan asylum and receiving two dollars a week as compensation. Neither is the sales girl's position coveted, unless in exceptional instances; but the position immediately above her is one of some dignity, and it is called head of stock. A woman in this position is scarcely less important than the keeper of a small shop, for she supervises all the goods in the department . . . and is altogether able to exercise her ability and judgement instead of being a mere machine.

The disadvantages of the lower positions, from the point of view of a lady, were physical strain and publicity; these jobs often involved standing for long periods, bending and lifting merchandise, etc. The saleswoman was in continuous contact with the public, having to adapt herself to their whims and needs; her work approached more closely to that of personal service than did office work. Both the publicity and the deference involved were considered unpleasant for a gentlewoman. Much of this unpleasantness could be avoided at higher levels in the same field. Where advice books are addressed to girls who were most likely to start as salesgirls, the emphasis was on trying to move up through the ranks as quickly as possible, into a more suitable job.

The job of buyer was considered the most attractive in sales work: 'One who holds a position above the head of stock is the buyer, and her place is so desirable that many ambitious workers have marked it as their goal.'[88] The descriptions of her salary, the interest and great responsibility of her job are so glowing that it achieves almost mythic proportions as a desirable job for a lady. It is discussed throughout this literature in complete disproportion to the number of women the field might have been able to absorb. But this unreality is less significant than the importance of the image it presented to women of 'dignified and pleasant'[89] work, unlikely to involve physical effort or unpleasant contacts.

The question of the publicity of her work was a very important one for a lady; the degree of contact with the public or with questionable co-workers was an important criterion in assessing the acceptability of certain occupations. At the most extreme, Ella Church argued that a lady could properly own and manage a lunch room, but not serve or appear in it. She could raise flowers for sale to florists, but not open a shop and sell them across the counter herself. 'The lady among her roses at home had nothing further to do with their sale, except to receive a handsome remuneration for labor that is in itself a pleasure.'[90] The character of one's clientele might make a difference; it was more acceptable to open a fashionable millinery shop than an ordinary one. And, the nature of the product might occasionally make public selling somewhat more appropriate. Even door-to-door selling was more respectable, for example, if one were selling books:

> It is a somewhat unusual thing to see an agent of any
> kind who looks like a lady or a gentleman . . . but a lady

who undertakes this occupation in a lady-like manner will seldom fail to meet with respectful consideration.[91]

It is not a calling that commends itself to the shrinking and refined; and yet in some instances it has been taken up, as a temporary resort, by ladies belonging to this class with very fair success.[92]

Although such fine reservations were soon outdated, the notion that public exposure and contact in work was unsuitable for a lady persisted. It runs through most descriptions of work in department stores, and it was a major reservation about telegraphy, an otherwise attractive new occupation for women.[93]

They are more or less public, and this is a disadvantage. Instead of meeting employers only (like the typist) the telegraph operator is thrown directly with the public. Exceptions to this rule are the positions to be held in large cities only, where the central offices of the telegraph companies employ many women.

In department store work, this disadvantage was compounded by the degree to which it appeared to approach work in personal service.

Performing personal or domestic services for people outside her own family was possibly the least appropriate of all jobs for a lady. It assumed a degree of deference and intimacy with strangers which was completely foreign to her standards.

It is difficult to recommend domestic positions to women who are born and educated above the class which usually fills them.[94]

The tip idea is obnoxious to gentlewomen, few of whom would care to go into a business where a part of the compensation came in that form.[95]

Domestic work, performing personal services like hairdressing or laundry, waiting on tables, were thus all highly questionable employments, although they represented many of the functions for which a lady was responsible in her own home.

However, although it remains clear that a lady cannot become a servant in the same way as 'the class which usually fills' that position, there was some attempt to specify the ways in which a lady might find employment at the same functions, in a manner suitable to her position. This necessarily involved some redefinition of the tasks so that they appeared familiar and reasonable to ladies:

> the lady's maid . . . has these advantages: she spends much of her time with a gentlewoman, she need only join the other servants at meal-time, and her work consists of such services as any one might render a sister or a mother incapacitated by illness.[96]

> Almost all of us at one time or another have assisted in drying or dressing the locks of friends or kindred. It was not a menial or unpleasant task. Then why not do it for a stranger who asks for the service, and who will pay a stipulated fee?[97]

> perhaps the first position suitable for a girl of some delicacy of physique is that of parlor maid and waitress. The details are such as any mistress might herself perform in an emergency.[98]

The argument is that these are services ladies know how to perform, and are used to doing for those they care for; if they perform them for strangers, under dignified and respectable conditions, it is not wrong to get paid for them. Ladies need not fear being declassed by such work, for if she is true to her breeding and standards, 'The superior woman cannot be kept obscure by her position.'[99] The reasoning in these examples may seem particularly strained, but it is an important illustration of one of the ways in which traditional values and experience were adapted to the pressing new necessity of self-support by women. These excruciatingly nice points and distinctions were very important in defining the ways in which it was possible for women to enter 'questionable' areas of employment.

A great deal of emphasis was placed, especially in earlier examples of this literature, on the ways in which a lady's training fitted her for particular occupations, or for following questionable occupations in an appropriate manner,[100]

> Much has been learned all the way up from childhood, quite unconsciously, in the shopping done for personal needs. . . . The best judge of household goods is a housekeeper, and of silks and millinery is the intelligent wearer thereof. So a woman starts with an equipment unconsciously acquired.

She might use this equipment in becoming a buyer in a department store. Or she might establish a small business producing preserves or baked goods, using traditional skills and a lady's particular knowledge of what other ladies need. She would, in either case, be supplying goods or services in which she had special competence, to a market she was specially equipped to judge and recognize, and in doing so, using both traditional women's skills and a lady's social training.

While these schemes may seem peripheral or impractical, they play an important part in the advice offered by these books, with as much space devoted to schemes for home production of needlework or food, for opening lunch-rooms, or growing flowers, or keeping bees, as is given to more significant occupations, until well into the early twentieth century. The precise, almost painful detail in which they describe these improbable possibilities is indicative of the desire to find ways in which a woman might *use* being a lady in earning a living.

This is particularly apparent in the discussion of what these books call 'artistic pursuits.' They devote considerable space to the possibilities of earning a living from commercial art, illustrating, painting china, doing portraits, singing, playing piano, or teaching music. What these occupations have in common is that they are all derived from the 'accomplishments' which a lady was expected to acquire to fill her time and enrich her surroundings, precisely because she was not expected to earn her living. Almost none of the advice books is sanguine about the possibilities of earning a living in these ways, unless one is specially gifted, has the advantage of serious training in a field, or an ability to teach. Yet the space they devote to the discussion indicates that many women must have tried to earn their livings in this way; Helen Candee felt constrained to warn her readers not to count on their artistic bents for anything other than enjoyment. There is something rather sad in the picture of so many women hoping to earn their livings through the accomplishments they had acquired because they were ladies and were not ever going to have to work.

Among the elements of work situations which were incongruous with being a lady, then, were manual labor, publicity, interaction with people of lower social standing, personal service, and deference. Perhaps the most threatening aspect of the working world, however, was the danger of falling into impropriety and sexual irregularity. The traditional guarantees of a lady's respectability had been the secluded and well-ordered nature of her social contacts. She was introduced only to respectable people, met them only in situations where nothing equivocal might pass unnoticed, engaged in activities which were without question womanly and delicate. Once she left this insulated situation, she had to be continually vigilant in maintaining her propriety. The *appearance* of respectability was almost as important as one's actual adherence to conventional morality, and women going out to earn a living were carefully advised to guard it. Some occupations were out of the question because they made it difficult to conform to conventional standards: 'There is a large demand for men as traveling salesmen ... but it is almost impossible for a woman to do this work, and a girl cannot consider it.'[101] Even in acceptable occupations, women had to be careful not to overstep the fine limits of propriety. Young girls were advised to be very careful as to the nature of any situation they entered:[102]

> When young girls go to apply for positions, they should be accompanied by some older person who can judge better about the character of the employer and the surroundings. . . . Too much care cannot be taken.

Women were advised to keep their business and social lives separate, nodding if they met fellow employees on the street, but not permitting more familiarity than that. Those who worked in offices were particularly warned about becoming too friendly with their bosses, discussing employers' home affairs, going out to lunch. Any of these might be the first step toward dishonorable behavior. Women office workers were advised to report any improper advances by fellow workers to their employers, and to leave if the situation were not corrected; but they were cautioned most sternly to make sure that they had not encouraged advances by any lapse from proper decorum.[103]

> A well-bred man is as courteous to his stenographer as he is to other women, and from all sorts and conditions of men whom she meets in the business world the *self-respecting* stenographer receives respectful consideration. (my emphasis)[104]

Eventually, a certain irritability enters these discussions, and the emphasis shifts from warnings of the dangers involved in working situations to admonitions about personal conduct. By 1919, for example, this was the tone of advice:[105]

> Much is said . . . about the snares into which the unsuspecting girl thrusts herself. . . . Of course it is always wise to be cautious but the girl who goes into the business world with her head full of stories of men who try to lure girls to destruction and all that sort of thing will be looking for trouble, unconsciously communicate that thought to others, and therefore may find it. . . . If a girl invites attentions which the majority of men are only too ready to give, then she has herself to blame . . . attentions are seldom proffered uninvited.

Women had to be careful of their behavior away from the job, as well, particularly if they no longer lived at home. Relations with men were especially important to manage correctly, in order to avoid the impression of being morally careless or loose. It was important to receive men in public areas – the parlor of a boarding house, for example, rather than in one's room – and in general to avoid any appearance of 'Bohemianism.'[106]

> You want to be a woman who is respected, not only because of her sex but because of herself, and the free and easy life in which a man offers a woman a cigarette . . . is one which my busy girl does not want to live.

Working women were advised to choose their acquaintances with special care, avoiding bad or fast society, lest they injure not only their own reputation, but that of working women in general.[107]

The details of personal appearance and carriage were very important. Since she worked, it was important for a woman to demonstrate in her manner and bearing that she was still a lady.

> A stride, a swagger, an air of independence, are a little fast and do not make you attractive; instead, only an object of curiosity.[108]

> When they are free and easy and swaggering in their manners, girls should hesitate before choosing such shop-mates.[109]

It was important to present a neat, clean, well-cared for appearance, indicative of one's self-respect and genteel background:

> Tears, worn places, and rips are never seen on a well-bred girl, for from her early youth she has learned how to wield her needle well and mend all her belongings with as much daintiness as she embroiders.[110]

> I have little faith in an untidy girl. She who goes without buttons on her shoes, wearing a torn skirt, a dusty hat, and soiled gloves, can never possess real stability of character. The learning how to care for one's belongings is almost as necessary as the learning how to live a good life.[111]

The determination with which this literature presses the necessity of presenting an appearance of quiet good taste and carrying oneself with the marks of gentility and 'breeding' indicate how fragile the claim of working women on a ladylike image was. It indicates that many working women had difficulty meeting the approved standards of appearance and manner; that large numbers of working women were *not* considered ladies; and that those who wished to be had to pursue their respectability vigorously.

The same concern is evident in advice to working women on recreation and enjoyment. There were considered to be many temptations for young girls living away from home, and it was particularly important to choose one's entertainment carefully. Again, the avoidance of irregular sexual contacts was most important. For example, dancing was in itself not unacceptable, if done in a private home or under vigilant auspices. But possibly the most consistent admonition addressed to working girls throughout this whole period was the warning to avoid public dance halls and clubs or balls for which people bought subscription tickets.[112] Since anyone off the street could attend, a girl might meet undesirable men and unrespectable women at such events, and be introduced to drink and fast living. The purpose of leisure activity was not excitement or unseemly enthusiasm, but mild entertainment, moral improvement, and rest from work, all pursued with suitable restraint and decorum.

Vacations in the country, for example, were advisable for getting fresh air and exercise, but not for dissipation and loafing. Reading was recommended – for light entertainment, moral instruction, the veneer of culture, but not for serious study or the development of unladylike 'opinions.'[113] Working girls' clubs were admired as sources of moral guidance, pleasant friendship, and 'chatting about light agreeable topics,' but Ruth Ashmore was disapproving of joining a club 'for which papers must be prepared and in which discussions are rampant.'[114] There is no indication in this literature of the passion for culture, education, and enlightenment, which one finds in working-girls' own autobiographies. Rather, the advice concentrates on pleasant, proper recreation and relaxation, mild social intercourse which involves no unladylike seriousness, and a concern with appearance. 'A girl's real character is revealed very clearly by the manner in which she spends her spare time.'[115] 'She seeks recreation that will rest her and give her pleasant memories without draining off the energy and enthusiasm that she owes to her work.'[116]

Indeed, a consistent refrain runs through this literature about how much energy and effort the working woman does 'owe to her work,' and how important it is to develop a businesslike approach to work. In part, this is a reflection of contemporary characterizations of the proper attitudes of workers to their jobs, of the need to introduce new workers to work discipline and identification with their employers' needs. But it also represents a tension more specific to the situation of women entering the labor force. The advice on businesslike attitudes coexisted somewhat uneasily with the detailed advice about ladylike behavior. While it was proper, even imperative, that women insist on remaining ladies when they went to work, it was almost equally important, if they wished to succeed there, that they should not presume upon their status. They had to be warned away from expecting special treatment or excusing inadequacy because they were ladies. It seems that, at least in the popular consciousness, women had brought some of the more incongruent of their attitudes into the business world at first, and had had to learn to adapt to its requirements.[117]

> The 'pretty typewriter' was the first of educated women brave enough to go down town and make herself a place in the world of business. She went timorously, full of feminine ways, dressed in pretty feminine fashion, and she was like a blooming rose tree in the sordid avenues of trade. No wonder they called her pretty when compared to the shabby office boy and the callow clerks. Since those days she has modified her dress a bit, adopting a business costume after the manner of men; 'down town' has grown used to her, and she has a dignified, permanent place in the business world. A frivolous girl will be frivolous anywhere, but there is nothing in the calling of typewriter that is undignified.

Evidently, women needed to be reminded of this lesson:[118]

> Another kernel of advice is to be business like. . . . Solely because we are women, we have got to excel men in being business like, that we may mend a reputation which was acquired during the days when Adam did the delving and Eve was permitted the luxury of simply being a woman of womanly duties.

They had to be instructed, as they left the world of informal and flexible relations in the home, of the more uncompromising requirements of business and profit-making.[119]

But in the world where labor is saleable material, hard
practical people will not give money for it unless it is of
the right quality, any more than you would buy mildewed
gloves or shop-worn hats at the price of fresh ones . . .
those who become paid workers must put away all thought
of sex and realize that in a contract 'value received' relates
to both parties, whether labor is for sale or merchandise.

They had to learn the requirements of their new world, then,
while preserving the standards of their old one.[120]

Sincerity of purpose, habits of industry, punctuality in
performing work, alertness in seizing opportunities, zeal in
performing the task assigned, and a willingness to do more
than the required task

had to be learned, and aligned with propriety, gentility, re-
serve, daintiness, and feminine attractiveness. No mean task.
　There was, then, a very detailed body of advice on how a
woman might work and still be a lady. Yet, despite all their
dicta as to what occupations were acceptable, how women
might enter new professions in a ladylike manner, how to
maintain the image of propriety and gentility, these same
books make it clear that many women *did* lose caste by working. Although the editor of *What Women Can Earn* argued
that a lady might now be 'secure in the assurance that she
does not sacrifice womanly charms or womanly privileges in
earning her daily bread,'[121] many of her readers were probably
not so sure.[122]

'What becomes of my social position?' ask those who have
not had their fill of accustomed gayeties. . . . Caste is not
lost by earnest employment; the world of society is not
cruel enough to turn a woman off because she has taken
up a serious and obvious duty, but she, on her part, needs
her time and strength for her work, and so there comes a
divergence of interest and a separation from all save the
choicest friends. But the compensation lies in this, that the
pleasures of labor are keener than those of indolence.

Despite the rationalization offered here, it is clear that there
was an important tension between working and being accepted

as a lady, no matter how many advice books one followed. Ladies who had to work were viewed as an embarrassment by 'society,' and found it impossible to continue with their old activities, whether from choice, as suggested here, or because they were 'dropped.' These books, of course, argued that it was possible to reconcile the two worlds, but the terms in which they couched their argument again make clear how thin a line the working lady trod:

> Society is wise in its generation. It realized not long ago that there were innumerable charming women within its fold who could work, and were ashamed to beg. Society could not afford to lose these women. Consequently it said: 'We will approve the woman who works, *provided she is a charming woman.*' You see, society makes the proviso.[123]

> The girl who works . . . need no longer shrink, hesitate, stammer, and blush when some one discovers that she earns her own living. Society, at first a little surprised at its own action, now gives cheerful recognition to the woman who earns her own living, but it *demands from her all that it does from any other woman.*[124]

A woman who worked was acceptable, that is, as long as her work did not detract from any of the conventional indications of her womanliness or gentility, as long as she could continue to maintain the appearance of being a lady.

Above all, this meant that she did not force others to recognize that she worked, and that she did not identify or think of herself as a 'working woman.'

> [Society demands] that . . . she does not discuss 'what happened in the office' at a dinner table; that playing a game is not interrupted by her opinion on bookkeeping, or that in the conversation after dinner she does not tell of the early hour that must find her at work. Society demands the result of the work, but not the history of the work itself. The well-mannered, well-dressed, tactful, agreeable girl is welcomed. That she is earning her own living is set down to her credit, but if she allows her

conversation to drift to her work she will quickly be exiled from good society.[125]

Socially, her work is secondary. She makes a great mistake if she is ashamed of it, and a greater one still if she continually talks about it.[126]

Even more offensive than talking about one's work, was insisting on the special position or problems of working women, or identifying oneself in those terms. Ruth Ashmore is scathing about the young girl who 'always managed to bring in something about the slights shown to the girl who works in an office' and offers this warning:[127]

You have a false little pride, too often, of wanting to thrust in the face of a stranger the fact that you are a working-girl. Now, what you are is nobody's business, and when you meet a pleasant woman and have a little chat with her, . . . there is no excuse for tossing your head back and saying in a half-scornful, half-proud tone, 'oh, well, I am a working-girl.'

The dangers involved in identifying oneself too closely with one's work extended to involving oneself too deeply with fellow workers. It was fine to become friendly with female co-workers or fellow boarders, but not to get too close and confidential with them. Women were advised to be polite, but not too open with others, basing friendship on shared pleasantness rather than problems, moods, or confidences. Ashmore is particularly denigrating of what she seems to see as an emerging working girls' subculture, characterized by an emphasis on 'chumminess' and sharing. She implies that the girl she is talking to is above the trifles and extravagances which attract more common girls, and that she will not be interested in friendships based on wasteful, flimsy standards. It was better to have a neatly balanced set of finances, for example, than to spend money on surprises or presents for friends. And it was bowing to an unadmirable desire for popularity to contribute to a sick fund for a fellow worker, who, if she had not thrown her money away on treats for friends, would not be in need of help herself.[128] What is clear here is that Ashmore perceived a developing, characteristic culture among working girls, which emphasized good fellowship, sharing, openness, spending rather than saving, and that she saw involvement in it as a distinct threat to a gentlewoman's standards and status.

This is representative of an attitude which was central to the advice literature: the insistence that the adjustment between being a lady and working was an individual one, possible for women of exceptional character and background, clearly above the common run. This emphasis did not have room, as indeed, most of the formulations in this literature did not, for the reality faced by the majority of working women.

By avoiding serious evaluation of the actual situations of most working women, and of the conditions under which they worked, the literature managed to describe an ideal *lady* worker. She avoided occupations which involved publicity, personal deference, manual work or physical exertion. She chose work which allowed her to maintain the traditional standards of the lady with regard to propriety, respectability, style, and manner, on the job as well as in her private life. The conditions under which she worked, the people with whom she worked, were expected to approach those with which she was traditionally familiar, so that the fact that she earned her own living became almost incidental. She most certainly did not think of herself as belonging to a class of women workers; her work was an anomaly, the result of individual and, hopefully, temporary, misfortune. Her status depended upon maintaining her distance from women who became 'drudges' or 'hereditary workers.' Working outside the home was a clear contradiction of her basic purpose in life – marriage and motherhood – and acceptable only as an expedient in response to domestic difficulties.

This image was very distant from the actual situation of the majority of working women in the period from 1890 to the First World War. Neither their family backgrounds and training nor the conditions under which they lived and worked made it possible for them to attain the standards or appearance of the lady.

It would be misleading, however, to insist that this image remained static throughout the period, which almost spans a generation. The years between 1890 and the beginning of the

First World War saw a major influx of women into the labor force, one which set the basic characteristics of the female labor force and women's occupational participation until the Second World War. This influx had a significant impact on attitudes about women and work, which is reflected in the later examples of advice literature.

The later books are somewhat more realistic in their discussion of who women workers were, their reasons for working, the range of occupations open to them, and the conditions under which they worked. Definitions of respectable work broadened somewhat, and standards of propriety and femininity were somewhat loosened. The image of the lady who worked blurred into one of working women who acted like ladies. The importance of work in many women's lives, and of women's work to many industries, was increasingly recognized.

I would like to discuss these shifts in some detail in the following section, because they are important for understanding the sometimes subtle shadings of contemporary attitudes toward working women. I will argue finally, however, that basic ideas about women's place and nature remained largely the same; that standards of female behavior and respectability were still very stringent; and that both still excluded the reality faced by the majority of working women.

The most striking shift is in the recognition of who working women were. This is apparent in the sense of audience which characterizes the literature. Earlier books had emphasized the unsuspecting and unprepared lady, thrust by misfortune or social reverses into earning her own living. After the turn of the century, advice is increasingly directed to young working girls, who, whether they work from necessity or from choice, do so as a matter of course, and because of usual, rather than exceptional, circumstances. The *expectation* is that many girls will work, at least for a period, and that their work will play an increasingly important role in their lives:[129]

you may be sure of one thing, that the day will come when you'll feel a strong desire to have money earned by your own hands, and to have a job of your own. You'll soon ask yourself, 'What shall I do and how shall I do it?'

It was increasingly accepted and approved that many girls might want to work, regardless of the necessity for doing so. 'We don't think any one of you would ever wish to be useless, for all girls when they grow up wish *to do* something' (author's emphasis).[130]

The growing importance of work in their lives, together with increasing requirements in training and skill for many jobs, made it especially important that girls choose the right occupations and prepare for them. In fact, most of the advice literature after 1910 is connected to the development of the vocational training movement. Much of it is written by teachers for use in public schools, and is directed to their grammar and high school students. As part of this movement, it insisted on the centrality of work in life, even in women's lives, its importance in individual development and the formation of character. It is dedicated to 'the girls of America, with the hope that it may aid them in *finding themselves*, their *life work* and happiness' (my emphasis),[131] because[132]

> Work must be more than a way of earning a living. . . .
> For the girl who does not find in her work itself a full
> expression of her thoughts and desires, no real life is
> possible – only a starved and stunted existence. Only as
> happy and efficient workers can we make our highest
> contributions to the world.

This is not a remarkable statement for a period in which public education generally reflected the need for recruiting a disciplined industrial labor force. But it is remarkable as a statement addressed to girls, to the extent that it expresses the idea that work might be anything other than an unfortunate necessity for women. This and similar statements reflect at least the beginnings of an attitude which admitted that women might have commitments other than those of home and motherhood.

The development of this attitude meant that it was very important for girls to choose the correct work, and prepare for it. The 'appropriateness' of work, however, was discussed less in terms of gentility and respectability and more in terms of the particular aptitudes and training of individual girls:[133]

> A glove or a shoe that does not fit well pinches and
> irritates the wearer, and this condition may be taken to
> illustrate in a small degree the chafing and irritation of a
> person who has entered upon a vocation for which she is
> not fitted: the stenographer who should have been a nurse,
> or the teacher who should have been a dressmaker.

Girls were advised to select the 'work for which they are best fitted by natural ability and training,'[134] rather than being urged to find those occupations closest to the traditional roles filled by women.

This is reflected in the wider range of occupations defined by the later literature as acceptable for women. Occupations which at the beginning of the period were considered highly questionable because of publicity, questions of dignity, etc., became more respectable. Contact with the public, as in sales work, telegraphy, travelling sales, was not considered as dangerous, in itself, as it had been.

There was a growing emphasis on the requirements of training and education for a job as *evidence* of its respectability. This was particularly true of nursing, for example, which had been highly suspect employment for a lady before the turn of the century, but is put forward as a thoroughly approved occupation by the 1910s. Clerical and other white-collar work received greater emphasis and approval at the same time as more purely ladylike occupations, particularly those which could be carried on at home, received less attention. Even factory work, under certain conditions, and skilled manual work assumed more importance as options and received more space in discussion.

Parallel with this wider range of occupations was an increased consideration of the availability of work for women in various fields, rather than just its abstract acceptability. Earlier books had concentrated on the appropriateness of various kinds of work for a lady, rather than on the relative availability of openings in the field. The discussion of department store buyer or personal shopper as jobs, for example, was totally out of proportion to the number of women who could possibly have been employed in those capacities. Later books were somewhat more realistic. They made some attempt to describe the availability of jobs in the fields they suggested; their requirements in preparation or training; and the general salary scales.

The most important change during this period, however, is in the sense of the social position of the women to whom advice books are addressed. Earlier books were addressed to *ladies*, women who were gentlewomen, but who needed to earn a living for one reason or another. The advice offered them was how, given the fact that they *are* ladies, they could do so without jeopardizing their social position. Later books were addressed to women or girls who worked, telling them how to *act like ladies*, how to meet standards of respectable femininity, despite the fact that they work. Both emphases tend to agree on what the essential qualities of gentility and propriety are, but the one assumes that being a lady implies a certain general social standing and position, while the other reduces being a lady to a standard of behavior which can be achieved.[135]

The earlier books make numerous assumptions about the social background, training, and connections which respectable women will bring to their work. Instruction as to behavior is directed at the novelty of the work experience, and possible awkwardness in adjusting to it. Ashmore, for example, is most concerned with warning 'her' girls against unexpected pressures or disappointments in a new and fluid situation where they might be tempted to behave in ways which would prejudice their claims to gentility. She assumes, though, that they do have such claims and know what responsibilities they entail. Later books, while they assume their readers are respectable, have far fewer references to the advantages of their background and connections. They emphasize, instead, education, experience, and training as preparation for jobs.

Their emphasis is on learning and displaying certain manners, attitudes, and standards of appearance which are 'ladylike' rather than on invoking the supposed original social status of their readers. They phrase the standards which they apply in judging work situations less in terms of the appearance of gentility and the maintenance of status, more in terms of a vaguer 'pleasantness' in surroundings and relationships with employers and fellow workers.

These changes represent to some extent the changing structure of the occupations women entered during this period, in particular the increased importance of formal training for some jobs which ladies had once claimed. They also indicate, however, a shift in the literature's conception of its audience, from one of upper-middle-class women to a much broader group. This is reflected as well in a greater recognition of women workers as a social group, rather than a collection of unfortunate individuals. Earlier books tended to see women workers as so many individual ladies needing to find particular ways of meeting special personal circumstances. The later ones tend to see them as members of a group whose options were determined to some extent by general social developments and circumstances. They discuss, for example, factors influencing the availability of work, the choices girls make of occupations, relations among women who work together. They do so in terms which make it clear that the working woman is in a situation she shares with others like herself, and that she expects to work as part of the normal course of her life.

Despite these changes, however, basic notions about women and work remained essentially constant. In a sense, the continuities of attitude which emerge are only the more striking in the context of the changes which did occur. This is particularly clear when one examines the discussion of factory work throughout the period.

As early as 1900, an article on 'Factory Girls' in *What Women Can Earn* recognized the historical importance of industrial employment for women:[136]

> Down to the present day, in spite of the continual influx of
> foreign labor, the factories perform the same useful service
> in giving employment to vast numbers of native girls and
> women of all ages. . . . The hours of labor, long as they
> are, are not so protracted as in domestic service, and the
> evenings are free. The factories are available for any
> woman who must engage in work and who does not enjoy
> the education and influence which would enable her to
> take up other occupations. Sometimes it is the only
> employment in the vicinity.

And in her article in the same book Grace Dodge recommends

that 'For a girl who is physically strong and intelligent there
is a chance of employment in large cities in the factories. . . .
I am not speaking of the "sweat-shops" of course.'[137] Later
books, similarly aware that 'this is the only field outside of
domestic service open to the girl who has to leave school at an
early age with an incomplete education,'[138] devote some detail
to describing the requirements, advantages, and drawbacks of
various kinds of industrial work.[139] However, as Dodge's statement indicates, the kinds of factory work and conditions under
which it is acceptable are narrowly circumscribed.

> The conditions in the factories are not always satisfactory.
> No girl can afford to work in a room where dangerous
> machinery is unprotected or dust is flying about. . . . If a
> girl wishes to keep her health and earning power, she
> must not enter a factory that fails to provide for her
> comfort and safety.[140]

> A girl should beware of unsanitary surroundings,
> deadening work, and low companionship. If she finds these
> in any factory that she enters as an employee she should
> promptly seek other employment.[141]

Factory work was acceptable, that is, if it was physically heal-
thy and safe, provided pleasant and interesting work, and
surrounded a girl with intelligent and improving fellow
workers. In practice, this excluded almost all the real factories
in which women were employed, factories which were consistently described by observers as unsanitary and unsafe, characterized by exhausting and unpleasant work and by abrasive
and often degrading social relations.

In fact, the only factory work which was described with
approval were jobs in a few model factories set up by a certain
kind of paternalist progressive among industrialists. The characteristics which made them acceptable were clean and light
physical conditions, benevolent management, and strict control over the morals and deportment of workers – something
approaching a romanticized version of what Lowell had been
like. The fact that all these model factories paid significantly
lower than average wages was not thought to diminish their
attractiveness too much. In such a factory it was possible to

take an ennobling interest in one's work, and even to find a particularly 'feminine' pleasure in it:[142]

> Their work [making paper boxes] might seem to be very monotonous, but the boxes vary so in size and shape, many of them being exquisitely dainty, that there is a zest and a pleasure in the task of each day. Then, too, it is the boast of the establishment that their boxes are the best that can be made, and the spirit, 'I will make this piece of work my best,' which . . . pervade[s] the entire manufactory, lifts the work far above the level of drudgery.

Women who actually made paper boxes for a living, however, described it consistently as among the worst work, and the most ill-paid, and the conditions in box factories among the most depressed.[143]

Cases of girls from such model factories who managed to save enough for trips, music lessons, books, etc., are cited to prove that 'notwithstanding the long hours and the somewhat monotonous routine, a well-rounded life can be lived by a girl who works in a factory managed in a humane and intelligent spirit.'[144] Even if these examples themselves were not rather questionable, they would still have been unrepresentative of the conditions prevailing in most factories which employed women.

They are important, though, because they indicate, by inversion, what the assessment was of most factory work for women. What emerges is the conviction that most factories were not an acceptable place for a respectable or feminine woman to work. In addition to endangering her health by heavy and difficult work in dirty surroundings, she was likely to find her sensibilities and intelligence deadened by monotonous operations. She was likely to find her moral standards assailed by low companionship, disregard for propriety in dress, language, and the manner of performing physical labor, and, possibly, by sexual pressure from unscrupulous bosses or foremen. It was still considered highly improper for women to perform most kinds of manual labor involving stooping, bending, reaching, and other overtly physical and undecorous motions, in close contact with men. Certain chemical factories, for example, are recommended in *Profitable Vocations for Girls* because women there 'have the advantage of working in their own departments separate from the men.'[145]

Thus, while factory work *per se* was no longer condemned as unthinkable for respectable women, contemporary discussion makes it clear that the conditions of most factory work rendered it so. While some of this discussion clearly includes accurate description and justifiable criticism of factories at the time as unsuitable places for *anyone* to work in, there is also a clear argument that these were particularly inappropriate places for *women* to work. In fact, descriptions of more typical factory work appear as a sort of bogey in the vocational guidance books, illustrating what happens to girls who do not pursue adequate training or education.

The only terms other than working in a model factory in which industrial work was presented favorably was when it involved the possibility of advancement and mobility. 'It is very important that a girl should enter a factory in which advancement is possible. . . . She must choose a factory that will offer her an opportunity to learn a trade.'[146] Some occupations which were inherently unappealing or inappropriate for women became somewhat more acceptable if viewed in terms of the possibilities for advancement. It was possible to accept certain jobs if they could be seen as a way of starting up the promotion ladder. The theme runs through all the discussions of factory work, in which lower positions are skipped over, and the emphasis placed on moving up the table of organization. Telephone work, for example, which was generally seen as unattractive because of the nervous strain and irregular hours it involved, was invariably discussed in terms of promotion from beginner to general operator to senior operator to supervisor to chief operator.[147] A girl who does enter factory work is advised thus:[148]

> After she has entered the factory . . . she should be polite
> and respectful to her superiors, ready to obey promptly,
> quick to understand and to anticipate orders, and
> observant of all that goes on about her. She will begin as
> floor girl . . . then she may be given simple hand work . . .
> later she will be taught to run a machine. . . . When she
> has learned to run her machine, the girl is in danger of

stopping in her progress . . . to prepare herself for higher positions, a girl should learn as many processes in her trade as she can. This she can do by taking work in evening trade classes or by changing from one position to another in her own shop.

Women then, could, acceptably take otherwise undesirable jobs in order to acquire experience, to prove themselves to employers, or to finance training for more acceptable work.

The discussion of domestic work was particularly interesting in this last respect. Working as a servant had been considered almost impossible for a lady; it continued to be regarded as unappealing and often demeaning work:[149]

> First, the girl feels herself to be placed nearly at the bottom of the social order. . . . Second. She has comparatively little time that is absolutely her own. Third. She must continually live at her employer's home, where she almost invariably is given the poorest rooms in the house. Fourth. . . . There is in all the intercourse of the other members of her employer's family with her a certain mental attitude which gives her constantly a feeling of inferiority, and this is destructive to self respect.

Still, it was often recommended, especially to girls with a minimum of education, in preference to factory work, even in preference to working in a store. Undoubtedly this recommendation reflected the need to recruit domestic workers in this period, which saw a sharp increase in, and much bewailing of, the 'servant problem.' But the arguments used to bolster the recommendation of domestic work are indicative of the importance of the supposed possibility of mobility in assessing types of work. The argument was that, despite its often unpleasant character, domestic work enabled a girl to save her money in a way that beginning positions in industry or commerce did not. Domestic wages were small, but they were free and clear, since servants received room and board and, often, clothing. In contrast,[150]

> The girl who goes behind a counter will not be able to make her expenses the first year and she will have very great difficulty in saving a hundred dollars a year after

she has learned her work; therefore, such experience is relatively not very profitable. . . . [Whereas domestic work] may enable a girl to make her own expenses and to provide for her own support. Such work is not to be despised, for self-support brings a degree of freedom and self-respect that means a great deal.

One book tells a little story about two girls graduating from grammar school. When their teacher suggested domestic service with a friend of hers as employment, one girl turned up her nose at being a servant and went to work in a factory; the second accepted. The first girl ended up working in various factories at poor jobs, and five years after graduating was still earning $8 a week, and working very hard. The second girl saved money easily in domestic service, took a course in nursing on her savings, and became a children's nurse, able to save $6 a week.[151] The moral is clear. Yet, despite the warning against false pride, the message is also conveyed that domestic service is acceptable only as a temporary occupation, in order to finance further training or as preparation for more prestigious work. The same book is quite explicit that 'those who must accept such work should seek to prepare for profitable employment later.'[152]

The same emphasis on the undesirability of ordinary positions and the importance of moving up out of them is evident even in discussions of more approved occupations like office and sales work:

the alert, intelligent girl . . . can be trained to become a high-class saleswoman. For this type of girl the store offers a fairly good position . . . if she is trustworthy, ambitious, and persevering, the department store offers a position that will lead to better ones.[153]

the girl who is bright, quick to learn and quick to obey, pleasant in appearance and manners and interested in her work, will soon be marked for promotion.[154]

The normal culmination of this process in saleswork, as in the factory, was supposed to be becoming a 'forelady.'[155]

When she has reached this point in her career, the
saleswoman is once and for all above the 'shop girl' and
may remain behind the counter or in the sales room; or, if
she has real executive ability and a good business head,
she may become a buyer.

In office work, the parallel process was achieving the position
of private secretary.

This emphasis served two functions – the general one of
encouraging appropriate work attitudes in employees with the
promise of promotion as reward; and the more specific one of
allowing favorable discussion of occupations which were, on
the one hand, the major sources of employment for girls and,
on the other, obviously contradictory of the standards established for respectable and feminine work.

Implicit in this attitude toward mobility and promotion is
the assumption that women remain in lower positions because
of some fault of character, intelligence, or ambition.

> The fact that the lower positions in domestic work are
> often held by inferior people makes it possible for the
> earnest and intelligent girl to secure prompt recognition
> for good work.[156]

> Subtract (the) bare cost of living from the earnings of a
> woman who occupies a place of responsibility, and the
> difference will be the *market value of character* . . .
> subtract it from the average earnings of the skilled or
> educated woman and you have the value of special skill or
> educational equipment.[157]

It is assumed that the girls reading this advice are the sort
who will get ahead, that they are the ones who will 'aim for
better things than the overcrowded occupations into which the
great masses of unambitious workers go.'[158] The emphasis on
inherited gentility and traditional social status which characterized the earlier distinctions between ladies and the 'other
girls' is muted and somewhat transformed, and the recognition
that working women form a distinctive social group is somewhat less uneasy. But the basic resistance to incorporating the
reality of most working women into the image of the respectable woman who works persists. The image has been broad-

ened and to some extent modernized, but there are still 'other girls' who are excluded. Indeed, their existence is necessary to the definition of who respectable working girls are.

There is no longer so clear a distinction between women who are ladies and those who are not, but there are explicit differentiations among 'classes' and 'types' of working women.

> Certain manufactories . . . have attracted a *very high grade* of young woman because of the excellent treatment and conditions provided. . . . factory work may be made attractive to the *best type* of working-girl. (my emphasis)[159]

The 'character' which a girl brings to her work becomes the important focus of distinction. A woman who 'worked her way up' to become a forelady in a shoe factory makes the point clearly:[160]

> Is the factory a bad place for a girl? Well I don't know. I do know that it's a bad place for some girls, and I want my sisters to finish school. In the end, though, it all depends on the kind of girl she is and the bringing up she has had.

Girls bring their own character to the work that they do, 'high class' girls elevating it, and the 'worst type' debasing it. The girls who became waitresses during the First World War were described in similar terms:[161]

> The type of women who have rallied to this work is distinctly a high class and their worth is appreciated. . . . Girls of this type naturally raise the standing of any occupation, and if more girls of her caliber tackle the job of waitress it will attain a real standing in the world of work.

Even jobs in domestic service could be elevated by the character of the women who took them:[162]

> The truism of 'room higher up' fits this case, although it might not seem so at first . . . it depends on the individual to keep [her] position humble or to extend its functions very near to the work of the mistress. . . . In all domestic positions the name of the place may be humble, but the individual regulates her own status.

However, in a situation where a girl could not determine the nature of her work individually, she had to be very careful of the character of the women she worked with. A major definition of what was wrong with many places of employment was the nature of the other employees a woman might find there.[163]

> The character of the others that are employed in the same shop or office should be taken into consideration. A fair estimate of this can be made by watching the workers as they leave at the close of the working day. When they are free and easy and swaggering in their manners girls should hesitate before choosing such shop-mates.

The definition of respectability becomes one which implies that a woman must either work in a situation where her individual character determines the nature and status of her work, or, if she works in a less individually malleable situation, insist on its collective propriety. In either case, the working woman herself is held responsible for the respectability of her working situation.[164]

> There are good stores and poor stores; stores in which the moral tone of the management and employees is high, and others in which it is not. No girl should remain as an employee in a store in which the physical conditions endanger her health or the general atmosphere contaminates her soul. There are high-class stores in which the faithful, energetic saleswoman can find satisfactory and lucrative work.

It was assumed that the working woman could, in fact, choose her circumstances, and that her situation was therefore an indication of her preferences and standards. However, most working women could not choose their employment so carefully, and many worked in situations which were considered suspect. By implication, their own morality and respectability were thrown in doubt. Remaining in a questionable situation was not necessarily considered an indication of actual immorality; but it was seen as evidence of a lack of that careful self-regard which would insist on the appearance of propriety as well as its substance. A more subtle distinction than that between the lady and the 'red-visaged denizen' of her kitchen, perhaps, but just as powerful in its exclusiveness.

This exclusiveness becomes even more apparent when we look at the actual social content of what was considered respectable character and upbringing. The advice literature did not discuss an abstract notion of respectable character and background. Rather, it proceeded from a concrete picture of what that background included, and what it did not. The basic image of respectability was one to which only young girls from solid, stable homes, of native birth and background, could lay claim.

The advice offered is directed most often at girls who can depend upon their families for moral protection and support as well as for some degree of financial subsidy or educational assistance. The image is of young women who are not totally dependent on their earnings for their living, who can live at home, or whose families can support them while they complete general education or specialized training.[165] Girls who had to support themselves, or their families, on their earnings, who were alone in the big city, or even the first of their family to come to this country, would have had a very difficult time living up to the standards presented in the literature. It was especially difficult for immigrant girls; the image of respectability is also very clearly an image of native-born girls. The 'other girls' or 'lower types' emerge most often as immigrants.[166]

> To work day after day through a long period of years with a great number of persons who are forced to live upon a much lower plane than that demanded by the average self-respecting American citizen is both difficult and unpleasant. A girl should inquire very carefully into the conditions prevailing in any factory before taking up permanent work there.

The girls with the standards and character which these books emphasize are American-born girls; the co-workers against whom they have to defend and protect these standards are quite often immigrants.

It is also clear that the most acceptable kinds of work open to women, the white-collar occupations, are possible only for the native-born. The emphasis on good English, pleasant appearance and good manners, in their contemporary interpretation, certainly excluded immigrant women, and often the American-born children of immigrants as well.

Finally, although the importance of work in women's lives received increased recognition and even approval in the later part of this period, the idea that woman's place was in the home as wife and mother remained primary. It became more usual to acknowledge that many women expected and wanted to work, but that acknowledgment was limited to the case of young girls working between school and marriage, or to women who never married. The attitudes toward the employment of married women, and the reasons adduced to explain it, remain strikingly similar to those of earlier periods. Married women, that is, worked only because of unfortunate and exceptional circumstances, and only as a last resort.

Unmarried women were in a somewhat different situation. It was more acceptable for them to work, and to want to work. In fact, they were often advised that as long as they worked, their jobs deserved their full commitment. Ashmore's archetypical girl, for example,[167]

> has asked me many times if it is immodest for her to long
> to be a happy wife and the mistress of a home, and I
> answer her emphatically, 'It is not wrong as long as you do
> not let this thought so fill your mind that your every-day
> work is neglected.'

The Girl and the Job even warns girls against the folly of planning their whole lives on the assumption that they will marry:[168]

> Don't think that when you enter the business world that it
> is merely to fill in the time between your schooldays and
> the seemingly halcyon days of matrimony which every girl
> believes are just around the corner. Give to your job the
> best that is in you, you are being paid for definite work
> and you owe it to yourself and your employer to give of
> your best to that job. No girl can definitely count on
> matrimony and even if she could, life will mean more to
> her if she has done her job in the business world. Too

many girls take matrimony for granted, it passes them by and they find themselves at thirty in a position little higher than the one they held at eighteen.

Yet the assumption remains that they *will* marry, that they will be unfortunate if they don't, and that despite the excitement and personal development which may be involved in earning one's own living, woman's role as wife and mother is her best fulfillment. Ashmore, despite her repeated warnings not to daydream over marriage possibilities, and her discussions of the possibility, even the attractions, of spinsterhood, still argues that 'the work done at home' is the most important work of all[169] and hopes that her girl 'still has enough faith left to expect to have a home of her own some day, possibly . . . with Prince Charming as her companion.'[170] Even the concentration of the vocational education movement on the importance of training reflects this attitude. 'The problem of helping the girl to prepare herself for a successful career, while at the same time enabling her to shape her life for her traditional home functions, is at once a delicate and difficult one.'[171] Despite the passage from it cited above, *The Girl and the Job* concludes that staying at home, helping one's family, or running one's own home, is the best job of all. *Vocations For Girls*, a book devoted to vocational training where 'The Girl Who Stays at Home' is a chapter about the exception to its subject, concludes that staying home is, after all, the best option.[172]

fortunate indeed is the girl who is not called upon [to work outside the home] but who finds her work in her own home. It seems strange that any girl should prefer office work and the business life to work in her own home; but the fact remains that many girls look upon themselves as martyrs if circumstances compel them to stay at home. . . . [Yet] no girl in an office is half as necessary there as is the successful girl in the home. . . . Fortunate is the daughter whose vocation it is to share in her mother's work, and to aid her in the making of a home, with all that the word implies of comfort, cheer, and love.

Not only the married woman, then, or the young woman

making long-term choices about her life goals, but even the young unmarried girl, is advised that her best place and most useful service is in the home.[173]

> Many a girl who has left a pleasant home, in which her services would have been of value to her own people, to enter upon tasks for which she was unfitted, has gladly returned to her own place in her father's house with the thought –
>   'Homekeeping hearts are happiest,
>   To stay at home is best.'

Conclusion

Despite significant changes around the turn of the century in Victorian attitudes about women in general and their involvement in the labor force in particular, contemporary ideas about women and work remained exclusive of the reality of a large section, even a majority, of the working-class women of the period.

Although there was increased recognition of the role of women in the labor force, and of the importance of earning their own living for many women, the basic conception of woman's role was that she was and ought to be primarily a wife and mother. Working outside her home was still seen as basically incompatible with that role.

Although there was a stronger sense of the emergence of working women as a definite social group, expecting as a matter of course that they would work at some point in their lives, there was still a strong reluctance to recognize the characteristic working woman in industries like garment or textiles, as a representative type. There was perhaps an uneasy recognition of the existence of such women, for whom work under deplorable conditions was a basic and determining factor, but no acceptance of their representativeness.

Despite some broadening and loosening of definitions of respectability and femininity, the standards of acceptability were still tailored to an image of working women whose character and appearance were supposed to be their own to determine. The level of necessity which shaped the appearance and behavior of working-class women was too raw to be accommodated by them.

Working women were, then, excluded from the acceptable image of womanhood and respectability shaped by the dominant values of the period. The question becomes, what was the impact of this situation on working women themselves? I want, in the following chapters, to look at the degree to which working women were aware of the dominant ideas of the period about women, and the degree to which they accepted them; to discuss the ways in which they responded to this ideology; and finally, to explore the degree to which they developed criticisms of it, and under what circumstances they did so.

5

Working women's attitudes toward marriage and work

In the period from 1890 to the First World War, the complex of Victorian ideas and attitudes, which shaped the dominant image of womanhood, had not yet come to terms with the extent to which women were entering the labor force, the necessities out of which they went to work, or the conditions and social relationships which they encountered as they did so. This complex of ideas was a very powerful one: in the generality of its distribution; in the official nature of the institutions through which it was promulgated (church, education, government); and in the popularity of its various reflections. It informed the appeals, directives and advice characteristically diffused by groups, organizations and agencies concerned with working women. Yet it was not, despite modifications and variations, an ideology 'adequate' to the experience of the vast majority of working women.

In this context, we turn to a consideration of the degree to which working women were influenced by this set of ideas and attitudes, and the ways they interpreted them in the light of their experience. The ideology of the period had two main thrusts: the idea that women's family roles and obligations were of paramount importance; and the image of the lady as the model of propriety, respectability and womanhood. In the essay I will examine the relevance of the first to working women: the ways in which they understood the relationship between the fact of working and the goal of marriage and motherhood, and their response to the implied (and often explicit) exclusiveness of the home and work as spheres for women.

In many ways going to work did mean leaving one social world – traditional, familiar and well-defined – for a very different one, with different, and often conflicting and threatening relationships, expectations and values. Certainly, the ideology of the period saw it as such, and saw an inherent conflict, for women, between the worlds of home and work. Social workers concerned with the problems of working girls saw the conflict as a basic one.

> [the working girl's] position at just this juncture is a more difficult one than that of any other young woman, for she is stepping out from the most old-fashioned type of family into the newest type of industry. This new social adjustment is just as inevitable as the economic adjustments that followed the industrial revolution.
> The working girl is stepping out of the most intimate, the most mutually conscious type of family life that exists, that of humble people.[1]

> The outside world and the home may become two almost antagonistic phases of her existence; at the very best the home is no longer the center of the world, but has become chiefly a place in which to eat and sleep.[2]

The world of work was a sphere of activity, moreover, whose organizing principles were vastly different, even contradictory to, those assigned to woman in her proper sphere. 'Interest and belief in the womanly ideal is likely to be adversely affected by the new standards of efficiency and power which industry holds before her.'[3] Women were likely to find the behavior and qualities required of them in the world of work very different from – often antithetical to – those which they had been encouraged to cultivate at home. Standards of efficiency and impersonality in work performance, and the unsupervised and promiscuous nature of social relationships entered into as a worker threatened to undermine the characteristics of gentle, retiring, protected womanhood. Nor was the threat conceived of in abstract terms. Because most working women were young, their entry into the labor force was considered a direct danger to their preparation for, and pursuit of marriage. At precisely the time when they ought to have been looking about for husbands (or making themselves available to men looking for wives), and acquiring skills for the arduous tasks of home-making and motherhood, young girls were devoting their best energies to earning a living.[4] The reports of social workers and industrial investigators echo with warnings about the lack of preparation of most working women for the demands of marriage:

> she does not look upon housekeeping as a trade to be learned, but expects to blossom into domestic competence after the marriage ceremony . . . the interest of the girl is divided between present wage-earning and future house-keeping. She has to look over a period of years before taking up her life career, and is meanwhile distracted by a largely or wholly unrelated wage-earning occupation.[5]

> Girls who go out to work at an early age have little opportunity to become acquainted with the domestic arts, and when they leave industry for marriage they are not at all prepared for the new tasks they have assumed. When coupled with poverty, such ignorance is disastrous. Home becomes a place of discouragement, instead of a strong defense against the misfortunes of life.[6]

Some of this concern undoubtedly reflected judgments about the quality of the homes from which working girls came – particularly if they were immigrants: 'Perhaps the fundamental fact is that not until girls come from something better than the present order of tenement homes, will there be a proper incentive from within to undertake hard work in the direction of preparation for marriage.'[7] Settlements tried many arrangements in attempting to make up the deficiencies: cooking classes and eating clubs, model apartments to inculcate proper standards, among others. Yet the dominant feeling was that there was a strong, if not irreconcilable, conflict between the girls' working and their ability to pursue (or interest in) preparation for marriage.

In addition to undermining the characteristics of true womanhood, and threatening the future of the home through eroding the preparation of future wives and mothers, work was seen as an attack on the authority structure and personal

relationships of the homes from which young working women
originally came.[8]

> The girl accepts the standards of the new world rather
> than those of the home. Not infrequently she becomes
> discontented with her home and ashamed of her parents.
> She chafes under authority, becomes impatient with
> narrow conditions . . . seeks freedom from home
> responsibilities, . . . and justifies herself by the claim, 'I
> am earning my own living and can do as I please.'

There was concern that young girls began to resist the authority of their parents as a consequence of going to work; and
that parents, particularly if of immigrant background, were
unable to cope with that attitude, or to oppose the standards
of the new world with anything near as interesting or rewarding at home. This weakening of family ties and authority was
considered a threat to the stability of basic social relations,
and the prelude to the erosion of community integration and
stability. More distressing, even, to some, was the consideration that the weakening of familial authority undermined the
major source and guarantee of female morality and propriety.
The lessening of her deference to parents' standards and stric-
tures as a result of going to work was often cited as the first
step on the working girl's road to immorality. This perception
by observers of the conflict between the worlds of work and
family, and the threat posed by the former to the latter, undoubtedly reflected part of the reality faced by working women,
and some of the tensions felt by them. In some part, at least,
the expressions of concern over the threat posed to the home
and family by work was more indicative of the brittleness of
the ideology which informed them than of the strength of any
real conflicts experienced by working women in their
situations

It is important not to overestimate the significance of the
conflict, either as a description of the real situation of working
women, or as an indication of their perception of it. Girls and
women did leave their homes to work, and did encounter new
standards and relationships as they went, but they did not, for
the most part, leave behind their family relationships and

obligations, nor their primary definition of themselves in those terms.

Going out to work did not mean, for most women, a sharp break with home, or being cut 'adrift' from family relationships. The vast majority of working women were young, between the ages of sixteen and twenty-five, and living at home with their parents. Even among those not living with parents, many lived with relatives. Investigators during the period were concerned to unearth the dramatic difficulties faced by working women living alone, and these tended to get attention in books, articles and hearings. Yet even determined seekers after 'women adrift' were forced to concede, sometimes almost ruefully, that there were not, in fact, as many as they expected to find, particularly in the sense of women living alone, cut off from and without recourse to family relationships and support.[9]

Nor was the connection with their families merely residential for working women. Working women and girls made significant and necessary contributions to their families' economies, contributing as much, and often more, to family budgets as women living alone spent on their own upkeep. Despite the rationale of businessmen, that girls living at home did not 'need' as much wages as adult men, the contributions of working girls were usually necessary to maintain the family standard of living. The evidence of observers is overwhelmingly that, despite exceptions, and areas of misunderstanding or irritation, working girls made those contributions almost automatically; accepting it as a natural and obvious responsibility. Working women felt their connection to their families very strongly, regarding it as the major focus of their social belonging and responsibility. Numerous reports mention the widespread practice among working women of turning their pay packets unopened to their mothers, who had in many families, particularly among immigrant groups, the responsibility for receiving and administering the family income.[10]

The position of the girl worker in the typical industrial family is rarely a desirable one. She undertakes self-support, and yet is seldom economically independent, owing to the custom invariably found among our alien

races of requiring the children's pay envelopes to be
turned in to the mother, while she hands back a pittance
for carfare and small necessities. The mother thus becomes
the custodian of the family funds, since the father, too, if
he desires to be considered a good husband, must give his
unopened pay envelope to his wife. Custom is insistent in
demanding that this be done.

Girls would turn their pay over to their mothers, receiving a
small sum in return for spending money, but being fed, housed
and cared for as part of the family economy. Indeed, this practice was of concern to some middle-class observers who worried
about the problems attendant upon women entering the labor
force. These, accepting the phenomenon as established, felt
that women would only escape their disabilities as workers by
accepting and excelling in terms of the values of the working
world – becoming business-like, efficient and ambitious.[11] The
practice of turning one's pay over to the family for administra-
tion was often seen as an old-fashioned even un-American,
custom which prevented the development of practical sense
about money and a proper sense of the individual independence of the working person.[12]

The other side of this pattern of contribution to the family
economy was the ability to rely on it for support during periods
of illness or unemployment. Many industries which relied on
female labor depended on the existence of these family ties to
support their labor force during slack season, and used them
as an ideological justification for the lower wages paid to
women.[13] The supervisor in a dressmaking shop was reported
by Helen Campbell to have told working girls, 'If you haven't
(sic) a home so that you have no expense of board, it is your
own fault, and I can't be expected to do anything about it.'[14]
Yet even women who could not claim the advantages of family
living in return were committed to helping in the support of
their relatives. Although most immigrant girls came to the
United States with their families, and lived with them until
they married, there were, among certain groups, significant
numbers of young women who had migrated alone, or in advance of their families. Living alone, or with a sister or
brother, these women continued to send support home to Rus-

sia or Italy out of their meager wages, either to maintain old parents or to help other family members migrate.[15] It is clear then, that going to work did not undermine the membership of women in their families in economic terms, nor their sense of commitment and loyalty to its members. It is probably more accurate to say that particularly for women from rural backgrounds, who had always been important to the family economy, working outside the home presented a way of fulfilling old commitments in new circumstances.

Nor did going to work necessarily imply entering a completely new social world at work. Recruitment for the industries in which most women worked often followed patterns of kin and community networks. Women from immigrant backgrounds, in particular, tended to go to work in industries already familiar to their compatriots. They found employment through family and neighbors, and often went to work in the same shops. Thus, particularly at the beginning of their work lives, they went to work in the company of father or uncle, older brother or sister, and often under their direction. In the early sweatshop days of the garment industry, girls often started work as assistants to older family members.[16] Even as the industry developed and rationalized after the turn of the century, its labor force continued to reflect these networks of family recruitment. At the time of the fire in 1911, the Triangle Shirtwaist Company, then the largest and among the most modern in organization in its industry, was characterized by numerous instances of family members working – and dying – together.[17]

The networks through which women obtained and learned their jobs in effect extended family ties and dependencies into their work lives, cushioning and often postponing the shock of transition to a new world with new rules and requirements. Entering work as one's father's assistant, as Rose Cohen did in the 1890s, meant not having to find or contract for a job oneself. It meant being under the authority of a person who had always stood in that relation to one naturally, and being insulated from some of the harsher aspects of the social relations of work, if not from the arduous nature of work itself. Indeed, Rose Cohen did not begin to think about her life as a worker until after her work life took her out of her father's protection in the shop, and she found herself unable to provide the protection she desired for her younger sister, then working beside her.[18]

In some situations, at least, a woman's first steps toward becoming a wage-earner were taken, in the first place, as a natural outgrowth of her traditional sense of responsibility to the family economy; in the second, as part of a network of family relationships; and in the third, often under the continuing influence of family supervision and authority. Certainly, this pattern was not often maintained consistently throughout a woman's work life. Changing industrial organization – as in the garment industry after the turn of the century – lessened the possibilities of entering the workforce under the direct supervision of family members, as the range of autonomy and discretion of sub-contractors and craftsmen was restricted, and replaced by more formal supervision. The instability and seasonal nature of employment in many industries which attracted women also increased the difficulties of family groups remaining together over extended periods. Further, the possibility of maintaining family and community relations at work varied for different ethnic groups and in different industries and regions; some groups placed greater emphasis than others on maintaining control over their women's place of employment.[19] Nevertheless, the penetration of family ties into the social relationships of the workplace did play an important part in shaping the work lives of significant groups of women. That such a pattern existed makes it necessary to use with caution the notion that women going to work necessarily experienced a sharp subjective break with their homes and families.

Although entering the workforce undoubtedly represented a new set of experiences in many ways, then, it did not represent quite so sharp a break with women's home life and family roles as contemporary observers feared. As they entered the labor force, working women did enter into new sets of social relations and demands, but they also remained tied to their families through residence, economic obligation, even the nature of their work itself, as well as through custom and affection. The degree to which they remained embedded in their family relationships is reflected in the ideas of commitment and social place of working women themselves.

Overwhelmingly, girls and young women who worked maintained strong commitments to their parental homes and family obligations. There is little evidence that the fact of working caused them to abandon or even significantly to modify their sense of their duties, status, identities as daughters, or the centrality of their relationships in the home in their lives. This is evident in the continuing deference which working girls paid to parental authority, the regularity with which they submitted to family discipline in social and financial matters, and the remarkable degree to which they continued to perform accustomed housekeeping tasks for their families after going to work.

Thus working did not really alter women's sense of their defining social roles and location, and they continued to function implicitly in terms of those obligations. In those few instances in which working women addressed the question of their commitment to the home explicitly, the same attitudes emerge. Girls in the clubs affiliated with the Association of Working Girls' Societies occasionally debated whether their club activities undermined their commitment to their families or took time which they owed to filling home obligations. All their arguments on the issue accept the absolute importance of their family obligations and the primacy of their relationships at home. Those girls who acknowledge certain conflicts between home duties and club membership defended the latter only in terms which invoked the home in another form – that is, they excused the time spent in club activities not because of its importance to them as workers, or for its intrinsic attractions, but because club life would prepare them to be better home-makers and mothers in the future.[20] Some members felt that this preparation represented the most important function of the clubs in any context:[21]

> It seems to me the most useful classes are those which best fit us to be *home makers*, for that is what we shall most of us be, in some sense. We need to learn the best ways of doing things and the reasons for doing them, if we are ever to make pleasant homes for our family.

Women who did not live with their families were particularly sensitive about the importance of the home as a focus of women's lives. Their response in that situation was not to defend their different mode of living on its own terms, but to assimilate it as much as possible to the traditional one. Thus, many social investigators complained of the difficulty of getting accurate statistics on where and with whom working women lived. It seems that women, when queried, would often claim to be living with an 'aunt' or other relative, because it was considered more decent and respectable to do so, even though they actually lived in rooms rented from strangers.[22] Such lodging, though, was widely reported as a last choice among working women, who preferred, if they could not live at home, to board with people to whom they could claim some family relation or tie of friendship. Failing that, they seem to have preferred rooming as a lodger in a family to the impersonality of working women's homes or the loneliness of lodging houses.[23] If they could not live at home, working women tried to approximate it as much as possible. They disliked arrangements which diverged from it too widely, even though these arrangements might be more rational economically. They did not want to repeat in their private lives the impersonality and individuality of the working world.

Another indication of the importance of home in their identity as women was the attempt by some working women to create 'homes' for themselves, even though they could not live with their families. Especially among older, better paid working women – who often tended also to be better educated and native born – there were often attempts to establish living arrangements which were consciously home-like and permanent. Louise Bosworth describes the strategies employed by women in Boston to establish living arrangements which they could claim as 'home,' and its importance to them.[24]

> This longing for a home, however modest and circumscribed . . . is almost universal. . . . Few working women, especially older women who have settled down 'into harness' and expect to earn their living all their lives, drop into lodging houses without a struggle for something better.

Far and Near, the magazine of the Association of Working Girls' Societies, ran numerous articles describing the possibilities for women to establish home-like arrangements on slender budgets. Usually, the articles were basically thinly disguised advice columns on efficiency, economy, and planning, but in one story, the underlying idea is made more obvious. Two old-maid sisters, of twenty-five, decide they are tired of boarding in other families and want a real home. 'I didn't choose my fate of being an old maid . . . and I don't see why it follows that I must be without a home all my life.'[25] After a predictably 'quaint' series of stratagems and adventures in finding rooms and decorating them, they are successful and happy with the results. The following conversation ends the story.[26]

> 'I love our home ever so much. I don't believe there is a happier home in the world, even when you include the truly homes, but I always feel as though I was trying to excuse it when I attempt to write about it.'
> 'Dorothy,' I said . . . 'why isn't this a truly home? Don't I do all I can to make it pleasant for you?' 'Why, yes, Hannah. But you know it is still the common belief to think "What is home without a husband," and generally speaking it isn't a truly home, but judging from our intimate acquaintance with homes it is.'

Even women who made no pretence of living with their families, and who had given up (in this case, it seems, rather happily) the prospect of marrying and starting their own, were still deeply drawn to the image of having a home. While the story is certainly also interesting for the slightly defiant assertion that women have a right to a home even if they aren't getting married, its importance here lies in the degree to which the imagery is still very conventional. Working women want, and have a right to establish, homes such as other women have, with all the emotional and status associations of the traditional model. The homes in these stories, those which Louise Bosworth describes Boston working women striving for, that the advice books dangle as possible rewards, that many working women express desires for, are not just physical settings, or a certain standard of material well-being, but represent a psychological or emotional standard which was still very traditional. Louise Bosworth recounts the conversation of a group of working girls in Boston's West End who compared experiences and came to the conclusion that,[27]

> the girls who were living at home had less money for themselves and less independence than their friends. On the other hand, they had an advantage which because of their ignorance of an unprotected life seemed not very valuable to them, in the form of security, companionship and freedom from the great anxiety of self-support. In reality the cost of board and lodging for girls living at home is far less than for those in lodgings and the value that they receive in return is hardly comparable.

The majority of working women were young and lived at home, accepting family authority, and acceding to the demands of family loyalty and the requirements of their particular roles in family relationships. Their families remained the center of their social lives, and their roles in it the core of their identities. To the extent that they considered the question explicitly at all, they recognized that centrality as right and proper. Those women who could not live at home tried to approximate the family situation as closely as possible, paying tribute in their own ways not only to the practical advantages of family living, but to its psychic and imaginative importance to them. Lastly, even the relatively small group of women who seemed somewhat aware that their situations did not, and would not, approach family living, reflected the continuing importance of the idea of the 'home' in their sense of themselves as women.

Going to work was certainly not without effects on women's attitudes toward their homes and families. Working, and the income that came with it, did increase the measure of independence available to young women, their sense of status in the family, and their position in relation to parental authority. Many young women did value these changes, and they were often the focus of family conflicts. But despite these effects, working does not seem to have provided a basis for a shift away from working women's primary commitment to their families, and definition of themselves as women in terms of their family roles. They did not, in fact, abandon these commitments when they went to work, nor do they show much evidence of believing or wishing that they had. Indeed, the most striking fact about their attitudes on the conflict between home and family and working is how little they considered it, explicitly, at all. There are very few examples, either in working women's remarks, or investigators' comments on them, of instances where they addressed themselves to the question of home and family as such. Where they did, they usually seem to have been responding to criticisms addressed at working women from outside.

However, working women did express themselves more freely on the question of work and marriage. In their attitudes on marriage and its importance to them, we can examine with greater clarity the continuing importance of traditional identifications and loyalties to women who worked.

That marriage and motherhood remained the central and defining goals of working women's lives is established without question by the testimony of contemporary analysts, social workers, and the comments of working women themselves. Marriage represented both the overriding achievement in the personal lives of individual women, and an institution which they acknowledged as of crucial importance to society in general.

Contemporary observers consistently note the eagerness with which young working girls looked forward to marriage, and envisioned it as the crowning point of their lives. Indeed, they were often concerned that this absorption undermined women's commitment to their immediate work. 'Instead of desiring to better her environment, she longs to be rescued from it. Marriage is her usual solution, but marriage with the imaginative hero who will place her where her dreams point.'[28] And they also worried that working girls did not have a sufficiently serious and exalted notion of the married state.[29]

> The majority of adolescent girls spend much time in
> thinking about marriage, very little of which is serious.
> The average girl sees in marriage a step toward freedom,
> or an opportunity to be rid of disagreeable work in the
> factory or in the home.

An overly romantic interest in marriage, and ignorance of its practical requirements, became a major component of the popular stereotype of working women from the 1890s on, particularly as it appeared in the I-lived-as-a-working-girl school of reportage.[30]

> Above the incessant roar . . . they called gaily to each other . . . What did they talk about? Everything, except domestic cares. The management of an interior, housekeeping, cooking were things I never once heard mentioned. What were the favourite topics, those returned to most frequently and with surest interest? Dress and men.

The ladies who publicized the experiences of their working sisters on the basis of a few months of what they conceived of as sharing their lot did not, of course, disapprove of interest in marriage. What elicited their comment was the lack of style, the impropriety and the vulgarity with which working women pursued it. Working women's concern with 'beaux' and 'steadies' became a staple of this literature, which enjoyed a certain vogue around the turn of the century.[31] An almost anthropological precision pervaded descriptions of the mating propensities of working women.

> The terms applied by these young people to each other will reveal their social level in the wage-earning world. If the term 'steady' is used where the world of wealth and leisure would use *fiance*, the under wage-earning world is reached. If 'friend' is used, the social ladder covered by that word . . . has many rounds.[32]

> The expression 'Who is she going with?' means who is her steady or beau?[33]

Such accounts marked the exceptionalness only of the ways in which working women expressed their interest in men and marriage, not that interest itself, which was, as Mrs Van Vorst remarked, 'the same as elsewhere.'[34]

Whatever their preoccupations about the meaning of this interest, however, observers all recognized its strength and prevalence; and indeed, they worried only about its excesses, having no quarrel with the centrality of marriage as a focus for women in general.

These characterizations by contemporary observers were condescending to a large degree, and reflected popular stereotypes. Yet some working women, particularly those involved in the Working Girls' Clubs, echoed them in certain descriptions of their own development. In one of the essays selected for *Thoughts of Busy Girls*, a club member wrote:[35]

Dear girls, let us think back to the time before we became members of the Society, and recall what our views on matrimony were then. . . . To what did our thoughts most frequently turn? What was the substance of our daydreams? Who dwelt in the air castles we built over and over again? Was it not the lover – the husband, who would release us from bondage and henceforth labor and provide for us? How our foolish hearts would flutter as we pictured him asking the one great question! How proud we felt as we walked into the workroom one day with something shining on our left hand that had not shone there before, and how important we felt as we grew to be the center of curiosity, alas, often envy!

Her essay is at the same time testimony to the romanticism of working girls' aspirations and an indication of the transformation of those aspirations, under the aegis of the Working Girls' Clubs, into a more practical and effective mode. She continues,[36]

All this only in fancy for us who are here to-night, which fancy was too frequently fed by sensational novels. It is a sad truth that too many brides forget the seriousness of the marriage tie, and think chiefly of the change from labor to supposed ease

and concludes with an assertion of the importance of practical considerations and serious preparation for marriage, 'this sacred, blessed relationship.'[37] Despite the undeniable influence of the clubs on her own and her co-members aspirations, marriage continued to be of central importance to them. Its salience remained unchallenged; only its imagery shifted. The goal of marriage was transformed from a romantic, unrealistic day-dream, fed by novels and popular songs, to the more sober anticipation of the duties and rewards of partnership-for-life on a middle-class standard. In either case, marriage remains the important goal for women. Indeed, one might argue that, in a certain sense, the latter model represented a stronger because more 'realistic' commitment to the institution. Overly romantic conceptions of marriage were dangerous in two ways. First, they set standards which were hardly likely to be realized in the situations of most working women, and hence to make them dissatisfied with the opportunities which did present themselves. Dorothy Richardson commented that the 'flesh-and-blood man of every-day life did not receive as much attention ... as did the heroes of the story books' from her co-workers, who loved gothic novels and the Laura Jean Libbey school of working-girl fiction.[38] Woods and Kennedy worried that young working girls preferred to go out with men not from their own communities, around whom it was easier to build romantic illusions.[39] Rose Schneiderman, later one of the most prominent woman trade unionists, remembered that in her adolescence[40]

> From the books I read I had also developed a special taste in men. Among other traits, I wanted them well-read and cultured. I never dreamed of marrying a rich man . . . [but] my idea of what a man should be didn't quite match up with the boys Ann . . . and I were meeting at the Saturday-night dances in the neighborhood. Most of them were loud and dull and suffered when compared with the heroes in my books.

But excessive romanticism was even more serious because it influenced young women away from suitable preparation for the marriages they eventually would contract, when they came to settle for something less than Prince Charming. Marriages made under the influence of rosy illusions and without sufficient technical preparation for housekeeping and motherhood were unlikely to be social or personal successes. Anticipation of marriage which comprehended a sober appreciation of its duties and obligations as well as its rewards, and stimulated an interest in technical preparation, represented a much stronger commitment to the institution as it existed, than did the intensity of adolescent romance.

Social workers and reformers who dealt with working girls were very concerned to promote what they considered realistic and wholesome attitudes about marriage, and they seem to have been quite successful in doing so among the girls who felt their influence. The Working Girls' Clubs under Grace Dodge's direction, and the numerous groups of working girls initiated by settlement houses, emphasized discussions of marriage and classes in cooking, housekeeping, and sewing as 'Preparation now for future wifehood and motherhood.'[41] Dodge repeatedly asserted 'that girls and women believe in homes, and wish to prepare themselves for housewives and Mothers,'[42] and that one of the most important tasks of the club movement was to help them do so through Domestic Circles. These included discussion of the importance and philosophy of marriage and motherhood as well as preparation for its practical side.

This was a continuous concern throughout the period. Almost twenty years after Dodge's comment, Woods and Kennedy summarized the opinions of settlement-based social workers:[43]

> The picturesque and dramatic aspects of housekeeping should be emphasized; constant insistence should be laid on the dignity of woman's tasks in the home; housework should be made a fine art and linked with all that is best in life. Mastery over its technique should be shown as an asset toward a really successful match; and a sane view of marriage presented.

Similar recommendations were presented at the Conference on Girls of the Association of Neighborhood Workers in 1916, for work with girls of fifteen to eighteen: 'Glorify home and their relation to it. Develop home-making instincts and discuss freely their coming responsibility in home-making and the efficiency and ideals necessary to the making of one.'[44] The activities directed toward this goal were quite popular among working girls connected with clubs and settlements. They claimed a large share of attention in descriptions of club life and in discussions at the conventions of the club movement, as in the following comment by a member of the Fall River (Mass.) Club:[45]

> To my mind the experience of our club has been that our success has come, not along the lines where we have tried to educate our girls, but where we have tried to give them, in the form of social recreation, a jolly cooking class, or an evening spent together over spring dresses and hats, that which might supply the lack of home training in the life of the working girl, and enable her, by and by, to be a better wife, home-maker and mother.

They were an important, and from all appearances, successful, aspect of settlement programs for girls at least until the World War.[46] It is evident in the preceding citations that the directors of clubs and settlements were quite explicit in presenting their reasons for suggesting cooking classes and sewing sessions, and in outlining their interest in promoting a 'sane' and elevated attitude toward marriage. Certainly, a good deal of the popularity of such activities must be ascribed to their intrinsic interest and immediate usefulness, but working girls in the clubs also accepted the rationale behind them. When they considered the question explicitly, they tended to echo the rather dreary views of the clubs' leaders on the psychic and practical exigencies of marriage:[47]

> A girl whose natural domestic tastes have been carefully and properly trained, whether at the Club or in the home circle, strives to make the home the most attractive of all places to her husband, and to carefully study his needs and moods, with an earnest aim to strengthen and help him with all the patience and charity that her nature is or can be made capable of. No girl who may some time take her place by a man's side to become his comforter and helper in fighting the battles of life, and become the mother of his children, the mistress of his home, can begin too early to know all there is to know of domestic duties.

They also tended to accept their views on its social and ethical importance. The directors of the clubs consistently presented speakers, articles and friendly talks on the theme that:

'Home' and 'woman' are words that go as naturally together as cup and saucer or hook and eye. One without the other breaks up a set, or spoils a fit.[48]

after all *home life* is the crown and glory of every true woman and . . . instinctively every girl contemplates a home of her own. As a rule this of course means marriage, for the ideal home is built upon a foundation of marriage.[49]

And these ideas also were reflected in the comments of working girls when they addressed themselves to the issue. In answer to the question 'Toward What Are We Tending?' posed at the first Convention of Working Girls' Societies in 1890, anonymous members of the Thirty-Eighth Street Club of New York presented the following suggestions, among others:[50]

Toward Strength and purity of womanhood . . .
Toward making bright homes and brighter children.
Toward the elevation of women in the public opinion . . .
To learn to become good members of home society . . .
Toward cultivation, strength, power and importance to the world at large. Toward happiness. The upraising of womankind. Union, improvement, progress. Toward making happier homes, better wives and mothers in all senses of the word, physical, mental, spiritual.

And a few years later, a club member reflected,[51]

In my opinion, marriage is a grand success, and the more mutual love marriages there are, the better for the community at large. Men and women are not marrying as fast as is good and healthful for public morality and social virtue. Pure, happy, virtuous homes constitute the nucleus of both Church and State, and a peaceful, united pair is the only normal divinely established unit of humanity, and the only true center and source of all that makes life valuable or earth blessed.

For members of the clubs, and for many other working women, both in and out of similar associations, marriage represented the defining social role for women. It symbolized the crowning point of an individual woman's life, affording her the opportunity to develop and display the most valuable feminine virtues. On a more exalted level, it was an institution central to the maintenance of the social order and public virtue. Written examples of working women's views in these areas were almost always elicited within the context of formal club discussions and lectures. In style of exposition, argument and example, their expression, with a few refreshing exceptions, testifies to the influence of club directors and lecturers on their development. Even the scattered instances in which working women voiced some resistance to the prevalent model of marriage tend to underscore its basic importance in their expectations and their images of womanhood. The most characteristic form which this resistance took, particularly among the children of immigrants, was the opposition to traditional standards and community pressure about marriage in the name of ideals of romantic love and individual freedom.

In Jewish immigrant communities, for example, arranged marriages were still very common throughout this period; where traditional practices had relaxed somewhat, parents, relatives, and neighbors were still intimately involved in questions of courtship and matrimony. Many young women, however, were growing more resistant to such customs. Rose Cohen describes both the series of attempts by her parents to marry her off, and her increasingly self-conscious opposition to them. 'But sometimes there were moments when I was tempted. A home! A piano! But was this all I wanted? And what was love? Now I know that I still did not know.'[52]

In 1903 Rose Pastor Stokes described the feelings of Jewish girls in New York:[53]

It is generally well known on the East Side that young men refrain from calling on their young women for the very good reason that the aforesaid young women may have 'other thoughts.' But . . . the average young man is not so much afraid of what the girl might think; he is more afraid of the neighbors and of her own immediate family – they are the ones who strongly entertain 'other thoughts' – a little too strongly for the young man's liking. And that keeps the young men away.

Naturally, our East Side girls are in despair. They have been rebelling in their hearts for a long, long time, at this very undesirable state of affairs . . . now, they have declared . . . that they are friendly to the idea of accompanying young men to theatres, parties, banquets, and other places of amusement. . . . The young ladies have formed a society . . . called the 'No Other Thoughts' Society . . .

Just imagine [a girl] going out with the same young man twice in one week and her mother not daring to take the young man by the collar and – (but never mind the rest) – just because her daughter is a member of the N.O.T. society.

What they objected to, though, was not the notion that they should marry, but the pressure to do it as early as possible, and what they considered excessive family and community supervision or interference. In a letter to Stokes' column, a Jewish girl from Chicago responded to a letter printed the week before:[54]

Although I am a little younger than that 'otherwise happy' lady, my parents are just as miserable about my present single blessedness. I am looked upon as the family *shlimele* and I have no end of trouble to reconcile them to patience . . .

When a Jewish girl is seen speaking to a young man but once, or once accompanies him to theatre, our good people congregate to celebrate their engagement. If a girl is past twenty and does not go out with a young man everybody calls her an old maid and those who are fairly acquainted with her will search high and low for a '*choson*' for her.

Women like this one asserted, in opposition to traditional arrangements, their right to individual, romantic choice about when and whom to marry. The letter cited above continued:[55]

It is every young woman's right to decide who shall be her life's partner. Who would tear that right from her and force her to a loveless marriage is – (inexpressible).

Let her wait and *work* while she waits. Let her grow mentally, morally, physically; Happiness will yet be hers without the aid of the *schatchen* [marriage broker]. It is never too late to marry, for one who well prepares herself for the noble duties which must devolve upon a wife, mother and home-keeper . . .

Hoping you will not embrace sorrow by submitting in a weak moment to the importunities of parents or *schatchen* who cannot be made to understand.

This romantic moralism was essentially different from the day-dreaming romanticism discussed earlier. It represented young women's response to the often bleak reality which they observed in marriages in their own families and communities, and which led them to criticize marriage customs in terms of a 'purer' love and greater individual freedom. Much of this response, and certainly the terms which they found to express it in, were representative of a much more general resistance on the part of immigrants' children to the 'old-fashioned' and restrictive customs of their parents. This often took the form of the assertion of individual rights and needs against the limitations imposed by family authority and obligation: many contemporary social workers and teachers commented on this tendency, and encouraged it, within limits. But the attitudes of these young women did also represent a response to their situation with respect to marriage in particular.

Nor was this response limited to the children of immigrants reacting to old-world tradition. The members of the Working Girls' Clubs were primarily of Anglo-Saxon background or the thoroughly Americanized descendants of the so-called 'old', North European, immigration. *Far and Near* argued repeatedly, as in this from its book review column,[56]

that no true womanly woman is, or ought to be, other things being equal, single from choice; yet neither does she marry merely to escape being an old maid; 'as if,' some one says somewhere, 'women were of no value unless branded with the name of a male owner!' Nor must a girl or woman marry for support, or for any other unworthy reason, though our author is by no means sentimental, and more inclined than some of us might be to make a place for the just-less-than-ideal marriage.

Marriage represented an ideal; it was not to be entered into for merely practical reasons, or to accommodate public opinion. If the 'course of true love [had] not been smooth or ended in a happy consummation,' it was far better to remain single than to enter a loveless marriage.[57] In fact, many discussions in the clubs touched on the notion that spinsterhood, though not a preferable, was an honorable estate. *Far and Near* argued the point in a story called 'Spinster or Relict?' Two little New England girls, playing in a churchyard, noted the inscriptions on women's graves and discussed their own futures: one declared that she hoped, whatever happened to her, that she would not die a spinster; the other, just as vehement, said she'd rather die a spinster than anybody's 'relict.' Of course, each was destined for the fate she denounced, the second girl marrying and the first losing her sweetheart in the Civil War. But the latter became a successful concert singer, and her life was not blighted like those of some other girls who[58]

> become embittered, and rendered useless and aimless by the idea that a rounded and complete life was impossible to them. How utterly foolish all this is! As if a rounded life did not depend on ourselves, not our circumstances; as if there were not always little children to sing cradle songs for, whether our own or not; as if humanity were not waiting for that pure love, which, deprived of its most natural object, goes out to meet and diffuse itself through other lives as a healing and heart-binding quality, losing its own identity in the identity of the many whom it loves and serves.
>
> Single lives, lived in the world, and for others, have their own special mission, as great in its way as that of married lives

A club member made substantially the same argument in more down to earth language:[59]

> It isn't half bad to be an 'old maid.' There are always younger sisters or brothers or nieces or little cousins to keep us sweet and loving, and one need not be a sour 'old maid.' Loving a little child is one of the best investments of affections (sic) there is. . . . Who is it that is always

called on to take care of the sick, and does it, too? Florence Nightingale and a host of others. No longer ago than our late war, it was mostly 'old maids' who braved the horrors of the hospital tents. . . . so hurrah for us!

Spinsterhood, then, had its compensations. It could be an honorable and honored situation, even representing, in some circumstances, a better commitment to the ideals of woman-hood than did a worldly or loveless marriage. Still, other things being equal, no woman ought to be 'single from choice'; and the 'most natural object' of her love remained a husband and family of her own.[60] Women might criticize the marriages they observed, or the considerations under which they were supposed to marry themselves, but they did so in terms which venerated the institution itself. They might accept the possi-bility of spinsterhood, and even recognize its compensations, but it did not undermine the place marriage held in their expectations, and in their image of womanhood.

Whatever form it took – the romantic day-dreams of ado-lescent girls or the sober ones of preparation for the practical 'realities' of marriage; the solemn contemplation of the insti-tution's moral awesomeness, or tentative criticisms of worldly considerations which tarnished it – what marks the instances where working women expressed themselves on the question of marriage is their overwhelming commitment to it and its importance as the defining role in their lives.

But most working women did not have occasion to produce abstract formulations of the role of marriage in their lives. Most probably never considered the question in general terms at all. The absence of elaborate ideological formulations, how-ever, does not indicate that marriage was any less important in women's views of themselves, or expectations about their lives. Rather, its importance was apprehended on the level of 'common sense,' the community's unexamined assumptions about the normal, 'natural' course of life. Young women and girls in widely varying working-class communities 'knew' that marriage represented the full achievement of womanly ident-ity, and were sensitive to its symbolic importance even when unconcerned about its underlying rationale. Rose Cohen, a Russian Jewish immigrant, remembered her reaction on being told by her parents that a young man had arranged to visit her, to get 'further acquainted': 'I was grown up, a young man was coming to see me! I would soon be married perhaps! The thought "I am grown up!" came again and again.'[61]

Women believed that getting married represented higher status for them as women, and expected to be envied by friends and co-workers when they could finally announce 'I'm a lady now. I'm married and don't work.'[62]

Working women had a diffuse, but real, sense of the importance of marriage in their lives, even when they were not engaged by considerations of its moral or social significance. But their behavior was only partly shaped by this attitude; their actual choices were also determined by the concrete pressures and necessities of their practical situations. Occasionally, these modified the basic commitment to marriage. More often, they reinforced it.

The commitment of working women to their families sometimes worked to mute, at least temporarily, the pursuit of marriage. The attitudes of working-class families often contained conflicting emphases with regard to women: on the one hand, they believed very strongly in the importance of marriage; on the other, children were viewed as important contributors to the family economy, and girls in particular were expected to demonstrate loyalty to the family circle. In fact some families were more accustomed to financial reliance on their girls than on their boys. Particularly in certain immigrant families, social workers noted, girls were required to hand over their whole pay packets, while boys kept theirs for amusement, education or other prerogatives tied to eventual independence.[63]

> The girls of the household are forced to give way unduly to the boys, and even go the length of supporting them in idleness and providing them with money to spend in saloons. Brothers hardly ever assume a fair share of the responsibility of keeping up the household, or caring for aged or incapacitated parents, or helping younger children. The whole burden is all too frequently thrown on the girls, who are impelled to overdo, and often to sacrifice the opportunity for a home of their own.

Certainly this is overdrawn, but there is no question that the 'underside' of women's identification with the family was often the placing of greater claims on her loyalty and the denial of individual goals.[64] Girls' ability to contribute to their families stopped at marriage, and families accustomed to calculating on the extra income resented, and could indeed ill afford, its loss. Parents, therefore, sometimes demanded that girls postpone marriage in deference to family needs; and resented what they considered premature marriage. Woods and Kennedy remarked on 'cases where the girl becomes engaged and extreme stress is used to keep her within the family for the sake of her income.'[65]

Some girls, anxious to escape their families for personal or economic reasons, and those who contracted early romantic attractions, would have experienced family necessities and pressures as a damper on their desires for early marriage. Others, less personally inclined to immediate romance or escape, may have felt the same pressures, but experienced them as 'natural' and right, obvious obligations which had to be taken into account in planning one's life.

Of course, family needs might also work in the opposite directions. Particularly when there existed the possibility of economically advantageous or slightly upwardly mobile marriage, early matrimony might appear a more desirable choice. Rose Cohen, for example, was at one point under considerable pressure from her father to marry a young man whose family owned a small grocery store; later he urged her to marry a small factory, sweatshop operator. In the first case, Rose described her father's interest in the marriage:[66]

> He was branching out, he was to be allied with a fine
> respectable family, with men of business. . . . It was his
> dream some day to lay down his needle and thread and
> perhaps open a little candy store or a soda water
> stand. . . . Now . . . with the prospect of having a son-in-
> law in business the dream looked nearer reality.

She also, at times, felt she owed it to her parents to marry, to get off their hands, since she had been sick and often a financial burden to them, and her father obviously concurred in this.

But this was probably the less usual circumstance. What we are concerned with here is not so much balancing the actual pressures on working women's decisions if and when to marry, as with the way in which they apprehended these pressures, and thought about the influences on their attitudes toward marriage. We get the clearest and most colorful sense of this from their comments on work experience and marriage.

We do not find large numbers of instances, as must be clear from the evidence presented thus far, in which working women articulated an abstract commitment to marriage as an institution. Nor do we find diffuse expressions of desire or anticipation of it as a personal event. We do encounter compelling evidence of the importance marriage held for working women, though, where their concerns were focused through more concrete reflection on the realities of their situations. It is particularly when working women considered the range of their actual options and alternatives that we find them expressing themselves on the desirability of marriage. The most concrete expressions of this attitude occur when working women commented on matrimony as an alternative to and escape from work.

Indeed, it is often hard to disentangle women's comments on marriage from their complaints about their work. Conditions in factories or stores were arduous and unpleasant, wages low, often insufficient for even minimal maintenance. The only escape from such conditions appeared to most working women to be marriage. A classic statement of the role that marriage played in the attitudes of generations of working women to their work is found in the song, 'The Factory Girl.' It seems to have originated in the Lowell Mills in the 1830s, but has recurred among female textile mill operatives in many situations since then. This version was recorded from a traditional singer who started work in a South Carolina mill in 1898.[67]

Yonder stands that spinning room boss,
He looks so fair and stout,
I hope he'll marry a factory girl
Before this year goes out.

Pity me all day, pity me I pray,
Pity me my darling, and take me far away.

I'll bid you factory girls farewell,
Come see me if you can.
For I'm a-gonna quit this factory work
And marry a nice young man.

No more I'll hear that whistle blow,
The sound of it I hate.
No more I'll hear that boss man say,
'Young girl, you are too late.'

No more I'll hear this roaring,
This roaring over my head,
While you poor girls are hard at work
And I'll be home in bed.

Versions of the song vary over time and from place to place, and its emphasis shifts, but throughout its history, the anticipation of marriage and its image as an escape from the mill, remain constant. Women from different backgrounds and in different occupations expressed similar expectations. Young girls, when they started work, were often encouraged with the idea that it would not be for long, that they would marry soon and escape the worst experiences of being a worker. Rose Cohen, soon after coming to America with her father, watched his drudgery, and seeing it as a model for the work she was soon to begin, asked him,[68]

'Father, does everybody in America live like this? Go to work early, come home later, eat and go to sleep? And the next day again, work, eat and sleep? Will I have to do that too? Always?' Father looked thoughtful. . . . 'No,' he said smiling. 'You will get married.'

Elizabeth Hasanovitz was another Russian immigrant, although she was older than Rose Cohen when she came to the United States, alone, and looked for work. She was given the same message, albeit in a different spirit, by an old 'forelady' in a Brooklyn sweater mill, who was jealous of her good looks.[69]

'Say, how long do you work in a factory?' she once asked me.
'Only a few months,' I answered.
'And I am working in this place for eight years, and I

worked two years before I came here. H'm! I guess you'll
not work so long, Sugar Face! You'll get a feller and be
married soon.'

There were positive aspects to the work experience, and
these were often clearly appreciated by working women. But
these were usually outweighed by daily misery and economic
uncertainty, and in that situation, most working women had
only their image of marriage as an alternative to turn to for
hope of change. Clara Lemlich, a young garment worker who
had played a key role in initiating the 1909 shirtwaist makers'
strike in New York, described the ways in which many workers
viewed their choices.[70]

> In the beginning they are full of hope and courage. Almost
> all of them think that some day they will be able to get
> out of the factory and work up, but continuing work under
> long hours and miserable conditions they lose their hopes.
> Their only way to leave the factory is marriage.

The desire for marriage as an escape shaped workers' behavior outside the shop. Elizabeth Hasanovitz noted the pro-
pensity of working girls for expensive vacations at boarding
houses,[71]

> they must appear 'swell' at those expensive country
> homes. . . . Fate may bring them together with a decent
> fellow in an expensive boarding-house; and there are
> chances of marrying and getting rid of the hated shop and
> eternal anxiety for a living.

The comments of less articulate women bear testimony to the
accuracy of these observations. A worker in a New York
paper-box factory complained that she was 'tired of doing this.
The only hope is to get married. It is easier than this, believe
me.' And another woman in the same occupation almost echoed
her words. 'I am sick and tired of this work. Stripping, stripping, stripping all the time, until it makes me dizzy. There is
one hope for us, and that is to get married. It is easier than
doing this.'[72] The attitude of an artificial flower maker was
described by her younger sister: 'She'd like to leave the trade
now, but she thinks that perhaps soon somebody will marry
her and she won't have to work any more.'[73]

Women were admired and envied by friends and co-workers when they managed their escape early. Sometimes these comments were off-hand – 'Ain't she lucky! She hadn't been workin' no time hardly before she married' – but they also sometimes revealed the full depth of what women felt they missed in not sharing similar luck. It was not just romance or a superficial rise in status that they regretted, but an opportunity for the only alternative they knew of to the factory's dead end. An engaged girl remembered her friends' reactions.[74]

> they looked at me curiously, and as I had once been envied
> for going to America I was envied now because I was going
> to be married. Not one of the girls had their families in
> this country, or a comfortable home. One spoke to me
> openly. She had been a pretty blonde girl . . . but now her
> face had no color and she stooped as she walked. 'You are
> very fortunate, Rahel,' she said. 'I am tired of the shop, I
> want something more than a folding cot for my home.' And
> she sighed and walked away from me with her shoulders
> drooping more than ever.

The tendency to see marriage as an escape from the shop or factory was engendered by the conditions under which women worked, and the lack of opportunity to improve their situation as workers. But the importance of marriage in women's view of their lives must not be seen simply as a result of the work experience. Disappointment in the reality encountered at work may have reinforced women's desire to marry, but it did not create it. Women's attitudes about marriage were independent of their work, and indeed shaped their work experience.

In fact, women's prior commitment to marriage was often seen as a contributing factor to the difficult conditions under which they labored. Some commentators argued that women got lower wages and confronted worse conditions than men because, expecting to marry, they did not invest time or energy in training and preparation for skilled work. Women who tried to organize their co-workers into unions often cited the difficulties presented by women's commitment to eventual marriage. A union of artifical flower makers, organized around 1907, fell apart within six months, in large part because many potential members expected to get married soon and could see no need for it, according to the women who attempted the organization.[75] A union secretary for the cigar-makers' union found the attitudes of southern white women to be the major obstacle to union organization among them:[76]

> they have been taught to think that marriage is the end and aim of their existence. They not only believe the preaching that 'woman's place is in the home' but they are ashamed to be caught out of it, and they are afraid to join a union for fear it will look like a confession that they may not land a husband and so escape from a factory.

While one might consider the south and southern attitudes toward women a special case, similar comments were made by union organizers throughout the country. Mary Anderson, originally a shoe worker, later first head of the Women's Bureau of the Labor Department, summarized long organizing experience in her autobiography:[77]

> A good many girls expected to settle the question of their future by getting married. . . . If they were asked to join the union some girls would say, 'Well, I don't care, I'm not going to work in a factory all my life. I'm going to get married.' Their great ambition was to get out of the factory. . . . In the days when I was organizing, the only security women could see was in marriage and that made it difficult to get many of them into the trade union movement.

Rose Schneiderman cited the same difficulties. A newspaper interview paraphrased her comments:[78]

> her hardest task is prodding the working girl to a realization that she should be organized. . . . But, say your Sophies and your Annas, we should worry about trade unions; what we're looking for is matrimonial unions. So with the aid of a little more lip rouge and the lace dress in the window on Grand Street, marriage is achieved and whoever wants the job in the waist factory can have it.

Yet it is interesting that, despite the difficulties it posed for them, women union organizers did not belittle or condemn that overwhelming commitment to marriage. Schneiderman concluded the interview cited above by exclaiming.[79]

> Not that I blame the girls for marrying – Heavens, no! But I wish they could realize that joining the union would bring untold benefits during the five years they are in the trade, not to mention how it would help the girls who come after them.

She was, indeed, openly irritated by the remarks of some middle-class women in the suffrage movement who bemoaned women's failure to develop sufficiently professional attitudes toward their work.[80]

> Frankly speaking, the average working woman . . . is looking forward to getting married and raising a family. Perhaps [professional women] disapprove of such frivolity, but, then, these are facts and girls will be girls even though they work for a living.

Other women organizers were also critical of the condescending reportage by middle-class women who took jobs for a time and then commented on working women's amusing propensities for beaux and fiancés.[81] Kate Ryrie, a Detroit labor organizer, attacked an article by two college girls who spent a week working in a collar factory in Troy, New York.[82]

> Very naturally the daughters of the rich, who are besieged by lovers (of their money), look upon the very natural instinct of the working girl to find a good husband as vulgar and silly. Let them change places with her in reality and not as a few days' slumming experience, and I'll guarantee that they'll be as anxious to get out of the factory by the marriage route as they were to shake off its dirt and get back to the shelter of their luxurious homes after their week's experience. They would then know the importance of the lover question with the average working girl.

Despite the difficulties it placed in the way of their organizing efforts, despite their often critical evaluations of the institution, and, indeed, their frequent personal choices to forego it, women unionists consistently expressed their acceptance of the central role which marriage played in the expectation of women workers. Although they often expressed this in pragmatic terms – marriage as the best alternative to poor working conditions – they really accorded it a more basic importance. For the significance of marriage in the lives of working women was evidence in the argument that, even though they worked, working women had the same interests, goals and desires, as other women, and the same claims to womanhood and its honor.

Such attitudes on the part of women whose identification with their work was exceptionally strong, underlines the significance of marriage in working women's sense of themselves as women. Although working women often expressed their desire for marriage in the context of complaints about work and the wish to escape its problems, their sense of its defining importance in their lives was more fundamental and pervasive. It is particularly necessary in this instance not to mistake the occasion which elicits the expression of an attitude for its genesis.

Lying behind the various expressions of the idea that marriage offered an escape from work was the implication that on marrying one would, in fact, no longer work. This reflected the most widespread assumption of working women that married women did not work outside their homes. It was perhaps the defining component of the complex of attitudes about themselves held by working women of the period, and its formulation offered the most characteristic way in which they negotiated the conflicts engendered by the intersection of their lives as workers and their position as women.

Appendix: the emergence of critical elements in working women's consciousness – precis and documents[1]

The previous chapter argues that working women responded to the dominant conception of marriage in the pre-War era by reinterpreting conventional values to accommodate their own specific reality. The conditions of their lives as wage-earners were not suited to preparation for the estate of marriage, and with it the assumption of a full womanly identity, as these were defined by the Victorian ideal of womanhood. Yet neither this disjunction, nor the disparagement of their patterns of romantic behavior which working women sometimes encountered from middle-class observers, diminished their attachment to the goal of marriage. On the contrary, working-class women felt that they could claim a womanly interest in this realm just as completely as could women of other classes.

In this way working women's consciousness was shaped through the adaptation of certain dominant values for women – including the maintenance of standards of female propriety and the aspiration for marriage and motherhood – to social conditions which contravened the prescribed requirements of womanhood. There was, however, an additional dimension to working women's negotiation of the conflicts of their situation. Certain groups of women wage-earners developed a critical response to features of the Victorian sexual ideology. The emergence of a critical consciousness was shaped by two key factors: social environments which fostered a collective identification, and the modes of organization which were created as groups of working women mobilized to change their conditions in the workplace and society.

The origins of their critique of aspects of the Victorian ideology of womanhood were linked to these factors. These sources included the anger working women felt in confronting the exclusive and derogatory implications of the concept of the 'lady' as the Victorian model of womanly identity, their rejection of the manipulation of this norm to deny their needs and legitimacy of public action, their discovery of new values of association and wider personal aspirations which came from worklife relationships and struggles, and their attempt to define their interests autonomously as they spoke out to demand necessary reforms (see documents 4 and 6 below).

In addition, their exposure to the well-developed radical ideologies of the socialist and feminist movements provided alternative social explanations to those offered by the dominant framework of ideas. These influences, however, were selectively filtered through the prism of working women's conscious experience. The extent of development and diffusion of their own oppositional consciousness was circumscribed in the end both by working women's continued definition of themselves in terms of central elements of the Victorian conception of womanhood, and the limitations of their organizational mobilization in this period.

The awareness of collective identity among women wage-earners was affected in the first instance by variations in their ethnic, regional and occupational milieux. Ethnicity was an especially salient factor that structured working women's consciousness on a number of levels. It operated not only in terms of generalized 'cultural' attitudes, but also through social relations in women's lives. For example, for young working class women of Italian background, cultural prescriptions worked on a direct level: group attitudes concerning female respectability discouraged Italian women workers from attending union meetings or striking. In addition, however, such group constraints were effective in inhibiting many Italian women from going to work outside the home at all, which was manifested in their preference for home work. As a consequence, large numbers of Italian working class women were not drawn into a collective employment situation in the first place.[2]

White native-born working-class women were noted for their concern to maintain standards of female propriety and respectability.[3] These attitudes were also sustained by a pattern of social relations. Young, white native-born women who worked for wages tended to be exceptional in their own milieu. They were likely to have friends not engaged in earning a livelihood who did fit the pattern expected of women, and consciously upheld an ideal of female domesticity. On the whole, white, native-born working women were less likely than immigrant working women to be part of a community away from work which reinforced their perception of the world, and in which they could see other women like themselves. By contrast, for certain groups (young Jewish women in the garment manufacturing centers, and women of Irish, French Canadian and other immigrant backgrounds in New England textile towns) the 'overlap' between elements in their position as members of an ethnic community, and their position as wage-earners, provided a greater basis for autonomy in their response to dominant social attitudes.[4]

In more favorable environments of this type, the crucial factor which crystallized an active self-awareness among working women was their own process of organization. The character of their involvement in two movements in particular – the rise of trade unionism among unskilled immigrant workers and the campaign for woman suffrage – both underlay, and set limits on, their articulation of a critical consciousness.

Consciousness change started from protests by working women over their conditions of labor. Their attempts to form unions multiplied in the form of scattered, localized strikes in the late 1890s and early 1900s. This wave of unrest culminated in the years before the First World War in the spread of general strikes in the garment trades (1910–13) which followed the great 'Uprising' of New York City shirtwaist makers (1909–10), and the battles waged by women and children textile workers in Lawrence, Massachusetts (1912) and Paterson, New Jersey (1913).[5] It is significant that none of the working-class women who articulated a new (feminist) consciousness of themselves as women had not also been involved in labor activism in one or another of these settings. Working women as a whole were concentrated in overwhelmingly 'female' occupations, and, when they organized, in separate locals for women workers. They encountered male resistance to their struggles and demands.[6] As a result, few of the women who were active in trade unions escaped some awareness of the special position of women workers.

The lasting advances in organization created new social ties and outlooks. Activist working women and observers from the Women's Trade Union League commented on the transformation in attitudes. Before unionization women wage-earners felt mistrustful, competitive and suspicious toward one another. Their common struggles brought a new ability to establish friendships and sense of identity. This was especially significant to the extent that the pull of home responsibilities on working-class women tended to isolate them and limit the creation of a tradition of collectivity.[7] Some indication of working women's feelings of warmth and closeness, and desire for continued contacts in the aftermath of unionizing campaigns, can be seen in the letters which they wrote to more experienced working class women organizers who had assisted them (see documents 1, 2 and 3 below).

Their acts of public protest placed ordinary working women outside the bounds of 'respectable' female behavior. These working-class women were told that it was unladylike to walk on picket lines, and risk subjection to physical harassment, criminal arrest and confinement in the workhouse in the course of a strike. If a young woman joined a union, it was assumed she had given up the idea of getting married.[8]

The efficacy of these cultural preconceptions forced organizationally involved working women to challenge the ideas of 'the lady' and 'woman's place' as barriers to collective action. These women refused to surrender their right to struggle for a fuller, more human existence than the one they knew of exhausting work routines and poverty.[9] In responding to the exclusivity of the Victorian conception of womanhood, some working-class spokeswomen started by denouncing the denial to themselves of the full attributes of a womanly existence (as defined by central values of that conception). But they also went on to develop a more basic critique of the dominant images of home and family that questioned the assumptions underlying the female life pattern prescribed by society (see document 6).

The participation of working women in the campaign for woman suffrage was linked to their articulation of a self-consciousness as women and a concept of feminism.[10] Their special version of feminist ideology differed from the vision advanced by the mainstream of the early twentieth-century women's movement. Wage-earning women stressed the contradiction between social ideas about women and the actual reality of their own lives, rather than demands for changes that they might envisage regarding their own role in society (see document 6).

The clarification of their own way of thinking in this domain developed from the encounter with opposition to their working outside the home, striking or demanding the vote. They answered defensively, taking the terms of this ideological conflict from their opponents, and shaping arguments against them.[11]

In this confrontation working-class women were responding, first, to direct attacks on working women; second, to general social attitudes which left them outside accepted social definitions (or worse); and, third, to difficulties which arose in the processes of organization in trade unions, and in their contact with feminists, especially social feminists.[12] The latter involvements led working-class women to a critique of some of the emphasis of the feminist movement, which they saw as coming out of the privileged position of many women in it.[13] Within the Women's Trade Union League, which was a key point of interaction across classes, personal and organizational conflicts surfaced repeatedly, reflecting class differences, in the form of criticisms of dominance by wealthy supporters, upper- and middle-class women's condescension toward working women, and the favoring of 'American' (native-born white) over immigrant women in its organizing strategy.[14] On a more general level, working-class members of the League began to define their divergence from middle-class feminists on the question of work and career. They rejected the concept of the career, and contemporary concern with women's professional advancement, as inappropriate for an understanding of working-class women's work lives.[15] And in presenting arguments for woman suffrage, they attempted to represent the position of working women out of an integrated, even if rudimentary sense of what they needed to fight for to protect their own interests. This approach constituted something more than the mere intersection of abstract feminist and class standpoints (see documents 4 and 5).

Yet this set of oppositional ideas did not systematically challenge, and go beyond, the framework represented by the Victorian ideology of the period. Furthermore, the critical perspectives which did appear failed to achieve a deep or lasting influence within the ranks of organizationally active working women. This superficiality of impact was related to the difficulties which these women faced in creating and extending adequate modes of organization to unite and represent their interests.

None of the existing organizations which channeled the protests of the early twentieth century began as, or became, the unalloyed expression of working women's own needs and consciousness. Labor unions, whether based in predominantly female garment trades or elsewhere, whether proponents of socialism or American Federation of Labor (A.F. of L.) 'business unionism,' were run by men on the national (and almost always also the local) level. Male unionists manifested a deep ambivalence, if not outright hostility, toward women's employment in industry. These labor leaders were consistently stingy in withholding essential resources from drives to reach unorganized women workers.[16]

The woman suffrage movement drew support primarily from broad ranks of middle-class women, although, after 1907 or so, sections of the movement curtailed anti-immigrant rhetoric, fashioned appeals to male working-class voters, and most important, enlisted working women in industrial states (Illinois, Ohio, New York, New Jersey, Massachusetts and California) in popular agitation. Even after this shift, however, there remained distinct limits to the commitment which the suffrage movement was willing to make to wage-earning women as a potential constituency.[17]

Finally, the Women's Trade Union League, founded in 1903 to help organize women into unions, was beset by internal strains between upper- and middle-class women 'allies' and working-class women members. These conflicts reflected the disproportionate influence of the former group. In sometimes overt and sometimes subtle fashion the allies' mobilization of their class-based resources imposed significant boundaries on the League's policy and direction.

Examination of the history of these movements, and that of the Women's Trade Union League in particular, suggests the insufficiency of either traditional trade unionism or feminism in the form of the suffrage movement as authentic representations of the reality or needs of working-class women.[18] Yet these channels of action encompassed the major forms available to female wage-earners who protested their conditions as workers and as women. It is difficult to see how a more adequate understanding of their position, or concrete strategy for guiding their actions, might have been developed at this time without the existence of a broadly based, mass organization.

In fact, the drives to establish lasting organization among women wage-earners were successful only in a few sectors, most notably in the garment industry. There the strikes of 1909 through 1913 in the waist and dressmaking, cloakmaking, white goods, kimono and wrapper, and Chicago and New York men's clothing branches laid the groundwork for the enrolment of 170,000 women in trade unions by 1920, or close to 50 per cent of all women wage-earners in the garment trades. This high level of involvement was unparalleled.[19] It was the difficulty in extending the early stirrings of militancy beyond the garment industry which accounts for the shift of the Women's Trade Union League from labor organizing to suffrage and protective legislation campaigns after 1913.[20]

An analysis of the shortcomings of the League, in this context, can illuminate the conditions necessary to the development of ideological and organizational forms which would have more truly represented the needs of working class women. Historians of the Women's Trade Union League have viewed it as the focal point of efforts to combine the struggle for working-class interests and for feminism on behalf of wage-earning women. These accounts have cited failures of commitment on the part of middle-class feminists and of independent strategy within the League as causes of the demise of this attempt.[21] This emphasis on organizational errors slights the more fundamental limits on working women's consciousness formation and mass mobilization stemming from social determinants of their position, particularly those rooted in economic, family and cultural domains. It also fails to recognize the necessary character of the League's double-edged role, given these social obstacles confronting working-class women, and the central importance which a mixed-class organization like the League attained in this situation.

Two of the basic limitations of the League's approach involved its concept of trade unionism (and relation to the American Federation of Labor) and the nature of its impact on working class women militants. From the beginning it proclaimed its loyalty to A.F. of L. principles, and sought to organize women workers into the existing (craft) union structure of Federation affiliates. This strategy proved inadequate and, in many instances, disastrous for the organization of working women.[22] The adherence of the League to A.F. of L. tactics was not simply indicative of a failure of organizational imagination, but rather a logical, necessary consequence of the class position of its non-working-class 'ally' constituency. Some allies, although honestly committed to unionization, and not in any crude sense manipulative, stressed the importance of developing a 'realistic' and businesslike trade union movement as a counterfoil to the dangerous and socially destructive possibilities in uncontrolled working-class activity, particularly that informed by ideas reflecting 'class hatred.' Allies' support of unionization thus represented different interests and social goals from those of working-class women activists. The League's conception of union principles was connected to the role it played, given this class basis, and the initiative taken by influential allies, in co-opting and training working-class leadership among women. The careers of the best-known League women – including Rose Schneiderman, Agnes Nestor and Mary Anderson – illustrate this removal of working-class women from the movement, and the drives to organize unorganized women, and their trajectory into government positions or legislative lobbying. Allies and middle-class suffragists used their control over resources and organization to make decisions as to which working women would have the chance to develop leadership skills.[23]

The shortcomings in the League's orientation and influence must, however, be placed in the broader context of the absence of a more effective mobilization of working women. The situational barriers which hampered this process were rooted in the structural position of working women in the labor force, the impermanent tenure of jobholding for many young women, the treatment of older women's employment as 'exceptional' and 'unfortunate,' the continued primacy of family roles in the social definition of working women's responsibilities, and the efficacy of conservative notions of 'woman's place' and sexual respectability in enforcing dominant standards of female behavior for working women.

The inadequacies of the strategic conceptions of the Women's Trade Union League, were less a prime determinant of the failure of consciousness formation in this period, than a reflection of the weakness of indigenous organization among working class women. The aid which some of the latter women received during strikes from non-labor women did not just exemplify women supporting other women as women. League allies used resources to which they had access as members of the middle or upper class – their money, prestige, or influence on public opinion. The Women's Trade Union League activities, therefore, neither represented cross-class action on the basis of a strong, independent presence of working-class women, nor, alternatively, an homogeneous feminism, based solely on a shared position as women. Rather, the League emerged as a crucial, often vitally necessary, actor in part as a substitute for working women's autonomous class strength.[24] In strategic terms, the difficulty confronting working women did not stem from conflict between 'feminist' and 'class' approaches on an abstract level, nor from a failure to design a better 'mix' of feminism and unionism in policies of the League. It arose, instead, from those factors of social condition and organizing dynamics which made the elements of an authentic, critical consciousness shortlived in appearance, and relatively superficial in impact, among wage-earning women.

What is interesting is that, in spite of these structural constraints, a set of ideas critical of the dominant conception of womanhood did take shape. This occurrence is suggestive of greater historical possibilities when social conditions support the organization of working women on a more powerful scale.

Documents

Letters from working women to Women's Trade Union League organizers (Documents 1–3)

Women workers valued the labor organizations which they created not only for the tangible economic gains which these achieved, but also because of the new personal relationships and the awakening of intellectual interests which they fostered. The letters to veteran organizers Agnes Nestor and Leonora O'Reilly written by women activists in fledgling unions shed light on working women's sense of the wider meaning of their efforts. In addition they express discouragement, and also satisfaction with hard-won successes, working-class women's eagerness to learn, and their desire for continued contact and practical advice.

Document 1: letter from a Philadelphia shirtwaist maker

In late December 1909 12,000 Philadelphia shirtwaist makers followed the lead of their New York City sisters and declared a general strike. Agnes Nestor of the Glove Workers Union was sent by the Women's Trade Union League to help. The shirtwaist makers won a settlement on 9 February 1910.[25]

LADIES SHIRT WAIST MAKERS UNION LOCAL 15
International Ladies Garment Workers Union
Meets every Saturday Eve., at 310 Catharine St.

Philadelphia, March 21st 1910

Miss Agnes Nestor
Bush Temple of Music
Chicago Ill.

Dear Sister!
. . . The standing of our organazation is good, very good, better still than we had ever expected to be. We lost very few of our membership. They pay their dues regularly. It seems as a whole that they have no more to complain. They have won in some measures materially, and on the outset I expect that this organazation will be permanently in its existence.
We have hired a new Headquarters. Everything is fixed up to perfection . . .
If there was any lose[r] in that brave strike! I was the greatest looser! – through my great activity I lost all hopes of getting a position in my city of Brotherly love . . .
Please write and let me know of everything. I remain Yours
[name illegible]

Document 2: letter from a corset worker

Beginning in 1908 the New York Women's Trade Union League, and Leonora O'Reilly in particular, had tried, with limited success, to assist in organizing corset workers in the city. In 1910 the corset factory in which Sophie worked – 'Mademoiselle Irene's' – had been the scene of a strike by seventy-five women.[26]

[no date]

Dear Miss O.Reilly,

I am very sorry indeed that I couldn't come to the meeting on Mon. night. The circulars were distributed at the appointed time in all the places but our's (Mad. Irene's) . . .

Dear Miss O Reilly I have been so discouraged about the corset workers lately that I began to doubt in the possibility of doing with them anything. But as you have much more experience in organising than I do.

Then please decide what remained for us to do now. I'll be up to see you Sat. any how.

Sincerely Yours Sophie.

Document 3: two letters from a Rochester garment worker

Ida Millkofsky probably met Leonora O'Reilly when the latter spoke in Rochester, New York in April 1913. In her first letter to O'Reilly, Millkofsky mentions O'Reilly's successful 'parade' – the great New York City woman suffrage procession of over 10,000 marchers on 3 May, 1913. O'Reilly responded to Millkofsky's request for 'literature that would be of benefit to me' by sending a copy of *Life and Labor*, the magazine of the Women's Trade Union League, and other reading material. Millkofsky indicates her reaction to this literature, and her views on the division of labor by economic class, in the second letter.[27]

40 Herman Street
Rochester, N.Y.
May 6, 1913

Dear Miss O.Reilly,

Let me congratulate you on the sucess of your parade. There is no words that can express my delight when I read how beautifully the parade was manged and the big numbers that turned out, nothing could pleas me more then to be with you and participate in this noble event, but as I could not be there, my spirit was there just the same. Many thanks for the books you have sent me. if you have any literature that would be of benefit to me I would be pleased to have you send me some. And I will pay the cost . . . The girls Local of the garment workers union gave a package party and dance for the benefit of the striking garment workers in Canada. We cleared one hundred and twenty five dollars which we think is very good, but it required very much work . . .

I remain yours fraternal
Ida Millkofsky

May 23 1913

Miss Leonora O Reilly
Womans Trade Union League
43 East 22nd street
New York

Dear Miss O Reilly,
   Your letter and magazine received. and I thank you very much
for your prompt reply . . . I have heard of the life and labor some
time ago. As they have wrote and asked me to be their sales
agent. As I am not a lady of leisure. and every minute of my time
is taken. so I could not take their propersition but . . . I am going
to prescribe for one myself. I have read the article labor and
leisure which I think is very good, as I quite agree with the
auther, for it is true that we need both things in order to meet all
that is required in life but the great fault with our present
system is that some have all the leisure, and the others has to
labor to make up for the work which they should do, but I hope
the time will soon come, when we all have leisure as well as
labor . . .
   Thanking you again for your kindness. I remain your's a friend
      Ida Millkofsky

Working women and the campaign for woman suffrage (Documents
4–6)

The involvement of women wage-earners in the suffrage movement
provided an important context for their expression of an awareness
of themselves as women. Their growing interest in the issue around
1911 led to the founding of suffrage leagues whose membership was
restricted 'to wage-earning women, to preserve harmony of purpose
and propaganda and admit of the greatest possible freedom of discussion at meetings.'[28] In New York Leonora O'Reilly was a moving
force behind these efforts. She argued strongly for working women's
distinct interests and claim to moral leadership in this fight.

Document 4: Leonora O'Reilly's congressional statement

Leaders of the Woman Suffrage movement appeared before a joint
hearing of the Woman Suffrage and Judiciary Committees of the US
Senate on 13 March 1912. The *New York Times* described Leonora
O'Reilly as 'the most determined' of the speakers. Her opening com-
parison with 'the lady who went to work at 18' refers to a previous
working class speaker (Mrs. Caroline A. Lowe).[29]

Leonora O'Reilly: Mr. Chairman and gentlemen of the committee:
Yes; I have outdone the lady who went to work at 18 by five
years. I have been a wage earner since I was a little over 13. I,
too, know whereof I speak! . . . You can not or will not make laws

for us; we must make laws for ourselves. We working women need the ballot for self-protection; that is all there is to it. We have got to have it.

We work long, long hours and we do not get half enough to live on. We have got to keep decent, and if we go 'the easy way' you men make the laws that will let you go free and send us into the gutter. (Applause.)

We can not believe in man-made laws any longer . . . You men say to us: 'Go back to the home. Your place is in the home,' yet as children we must come out of the home at 11, at 13, and at 15 years of age to earn a living; we have got to make good or starve.

'Pay your way' we are taught in school and in church . . . Well, if any people on earth pay their way in life we working women do. The return we get is that most of us become physical wrecks along the roadside of life. When you gentlemen hear what it costs a working woman to 'pay her way' in life, you sit back in your chairs, say 'the story is terrible, but they manage to live somehow.' Somehow-that is it, gentlemen. I want to make you realize the somehow of life to the hundreds of girls I have seen go down in the struggle. You men do not care . . .

Now, while we have had the colleges opened to women, only one woman in a thousand goes to college, while modern industry claims one woman in every five today. It is industrial methods which are teaching the women the facts I am telling you. 'Do the other fellow before he gets a chance to do you' – do him so hard that he can not stand up again; that is good business. We know that, and we women are sure that there must be some higher standard for life than business.

We are not getting a square deal; we go before legislature after legislature to tell our story, but they fail to help the women who are being speeded so high in the mills and in factories, from 54 hours to 72 hours in stores in New York, and 92 hours in one week in subcellar laundries. Who cares! Nobody! . . . nobody cares about making laws so long as we get cheap and nasty things in the market . . .

We working women want the ballot, not as a privilege, but as a right. You say you have only given the ballot as an expediency; you have never given it as a right; then we demand it as an expediency for the 8,000,000 working women. All the other women ought to have it, but we working women *must* have it. (Applause.)

Document 5: suffrage leaflet

The leaflets of the New York Wage-Earners' Suffrage League translated Leonora O'Reilly's message into a straightforward appeal to the immediate interests of working-class women.[30]

WHY?

Why are you paid less than a man?
Why do you work in a fire-trap?
Why are your hours so long?
Why are you all strap hangers when you pay for a seat?
Why do you pay the most rent for the worst houses?
Why does the cost of living go up while wages go down?
Why do your children go into factories?
Why do you eat adulterated food?
Why don't you get a square deal in the courts?
  Because you are a woman and have no vote.
      Votes make the law.
      Votes enforce the law.
    The law controls conditions.
Women who want better conditions MUST vote.
    Join the Wage-Earners' Suffrage League
  Meetings the Second and Fourth Monday of every month
      at 8 P.M.
At Headquarters, Room 212 Metropolitan Tower
    Fee: Ten Cents a month.

Document 6: 'senators vs. working women': speeches of Rose Schneiderman and Clara Lemlich

One of the most significant aspects of women wage-earners' activity for suffrage was that it brought them in conflict with conservative spokesmen who invoked a sentimentalized ideal of womanhood, and implicitly denigrated the womanliness and real needs of working-class women. The statements by antisuffrage state senators provoked a sharp response at a meeting held jointly by middle-class collegiate and working women in April 1912. The public leadership taken by working-class women in this suffrage event and critical substance of their public stance were unprecedented. The *New York Times* called it 'a gathering unique in . . . [Cooper Union's] history,' and quoted Leonora O'Reilly, who said after the meeting, 'The world is beginning to understand what it owes to the working woman. . . . Women who have had education in colleges have come here tonite to act as ushers for working women. Take it home and dream about it. . .'. The following excerpts include the introduction published in the Wage-Earners' Suffrage League pamphlet containing the speeches.[31]

Miss Rose Schneiderman, Cap Maker, 'Delicacy and Charm of Women'

The futile sentimentality of a number of the New York Senators and Assemblymen was put to the blush and the laugh at Cooper Union on the evening of April 22, when an inspiring mass meeting was held under the joint auspices of the Wage Earners' and the Collegiate Equal Suffrage Leagues. The College Women, in caps and gowns, acted as ushers for the meeting, and Mrs. Charles Tiffany on their behalf handed the meeting over to Miss Leonora O'Reilly, President of the Wage Earners' Suffrage League. She marshaled a squad of practical working women who presented their views with such convincing directness that they were compelled to return to the front of the platform and bow several times in response to the enthusiastic applause. Young women who have stood for betterment of conditions in their respective trades, each took a quotation from speeches of law-makers setting forth obsolete quibbles why women should not vote and made reply.

Rose Schneiderman, Cap Maker, answers the New York Senator who says:

'Get women into the arena of politics with its alliances and distressing contests – the delicacy is gone, the charm is gone, and you emasculize women.'

. . . Perhaps, working women are not regarded as women, because it seems to me, when they talk all this trash of theirs about finer qualities and 'man's admiration and devotion to the sex' – 'Cornelia's Jewels' – 'Preserving Motherhood' – 'Woman's duty to minister to man in the home' – 'The delicacy and charm of women being gone,' they cannot mean the working women. We have 800,000 women in New York State who go out into the industrial world, not through any choice of their own, but because necessity forces them out to earn their daily bread.

. . . We have women working in the foundries, stripped to the waist, if you please, because of the heat. *Yet the Senator says nothing about these women losing their charm.* They have got to retain their charm and delicacy and work in foundries. Of course, you know the reason they are employed in foundries is that they are cheaper and work longer hours than men.

Women in laundries, for instance, stand for 13 or 14 hours in the terrible steam and heat with their hands in hot starch. Surely these women won't lose any more of their beauty and charm by putting a ballot in a ballot box once a year than they are likely to lose standing in foundries or laundries all year round.

. . . It seems to me that the working women ought to wake up to the truth of the situation; all this talk about women's charm does not mean working women. Working women are expected to work and produce their kind so that they, too, may work until they die of some industrial disease.

We hear our anti-suffragettes saying, 'Why, when you get the vote it will hinder you from doing welfare work, doing uplift work.' Who are they going to uplift? Is it you and I they want to uplift? I think if they would lift themselves off our shoulders they would be doing a better bit of useful work. I think you know by

now that if the workers got what they earn there would be no
need of uplift work and welfare work or anything of that kind.

. . . It is too ridiculous, this talk of becoming less womanly, just
as if a woman could be anything else except a woman.

Miss Clara Lemlich, Shirt-Waist Maker, 'Relieving Working
Women of the Burdens and Responsibility of Life'

Let us look for a moment to see what happens when . . . young
girls go into factories. In the beginning they are full of courage
and hope. . . . Continuing to work in the factory under the long
hours, miserable conditions . . . they lose their courage. . . . Many
a girl who has worked for years at a machine, trying to live
decently, at last sees the only way to get out of the factory is to
think of marriage. . . . She is ready to give herself to any man
who will make the offer! Well, sometimes she gets a man who
offers to marry her, but I am sorry to say that there are
thousands of our working girls who are soon disappointed,
because . . . right after they are married, they have to go back
into the factory because their husbands are not making enough to
keep them; out she goes to the factory to help carry *man's burden
as well as her own*. When she has children, she has to be the
mother to the children, the housekeeper, if you please, and go to
the factory as well. Of course, she regrets it, but it is a little too
late.

. . . Men carry the burden; it's a joke! Have you heard him
object to stay home and attend to the children? Do you know of
any that do it? I don't. Out she goes to the factory and into the
office buildings to clean. You can see them at midnight; just go
through any of the public buildings, you will see those old,
middle aged women on their knees scrubbing the dirt that men of
business have brought in during the day. That gives you a
picture of how well men carry the burdens of women.

What about the unmarried girls? We have now thousands of
girls in the ranks of the workers who have not married, or who
have never had a chance to marry. What about them? Has any
man carried their burden?

I have met at least one who says that someone carried the
burden for her to her sorrow in the end.

We are told that we have 31,000 women over the age of 65
years that are self-supporting. I wonder if the Senator, who got
off that admirable phrase, knows about these women? . . .

Men say they want to *relieve us of the responsibilities of life*.
Well, men, you are responsible for a great many of our burdens.
For the 30,000 prostitutes that we have in New York City alone,
you men are responsible. Every man is responsible for the ruin of
every woman. You men as a body, men who make the laws, and
men of money who support the makers of the law are responsible

for this system of ours that forces 30,000 girls out into the streets to earn their living. (Applause). You know that when the girls are brought to court, to a court of men, they are punished. They are fined and punished for the sins of men.

There are two moralities – one for men and one for women.

Have you noticed that when a man comes across a fallen women, what he does to take the burden off her back? Does he claim that he is responsible, or acknowledge, at least, that men are responsible? Does he help her? Does he relieve her? No. He takes advantage of her, if possible. If she becomes a woman of the streets she is arrested, the judge fines her, and the woman who has no other means of getting money to pay her fine has to go out and sell herself again in order to pay the court. That is man's protection of unfortunate women every time.

Well, the Senator who said the reason he wants to keep women from getting the vote is because *he wants to relieve women of the burdens and responsibilities of life* may be thinking of some glorious time in the future when women won't have to eat – then they won't need to sell themselves – maybe he has a dream like this, but can he make his dream come true?

In my trade, the shirt-waist industry, it is said, that we have about 200,000 people working, only 5 per cent of them are men. Can you think of this shirt-waist industry without this 175,000 women? And the shirt-waist industry is not the only one that needs women's labor. All the mills, or at least most of them, employ women only, and many other trades which I need not mention here.

How would the Senator get rid of us? How would he help women? He cannot help us. *We must help ourselves.*

. . . Does this Senator think that we workers, men and women, do not know that every class that ever lived on another always told the slaves that it was good for them to be slaves?

Man as a class has ruled women.

He wants to make her think it is for her good he rules her, but it is too late. We are here, Senators, we are here, we are here 800,000 women in New York State alone. We have learned a good many other things. We have learned to organize in the industrial field. We have not learned to make good in the political field yet, but give us a chance.

. . . The working women, together with the working man, through an intelligent vote, *mind you, through an intelligent vote*, you know what that means, will make this industrial and political world over into a place where there will be less burdens and more happiness for all.

Afterword

Nancy F. Cott

It is fairly well understood, by those who care to learn, that sex discrimination and sex segregation affect all women's experience of paid work, from the most menial wage-earner to the most elevated professional, though in varying kinds and degrees. Sex segregation is perhaps the most striking characteristic of the labor market, more evident now that a greater proportion of women are in it: with few exceptions, women are hired to do 'women's work,' men, 'men's,' and the general assumption and practice are that women can't do men's work and men won't do women's. One might view occupational sex segregation with equanimity were it not that 'women's work,' since the onset of industrialization, has been synonymous with jobs of lower skill, lower pay, greater turnover, and less structure or opportunity for advancement. And the imposing legacy of the American Federation of Labor, characterized by early emphasis on skilled work and craft unions (which left women out), together with complex factors of women workers' age, skills, transiency and expectations of marriage, have led proportionately fewer women workers into trade unions, in a nation in which the proportion of organized male workers is notably low.

Yet in contrast to the dismal litany of women's secondary place in the paid labor force, wage-earning as it became the predominant form of 'making a living' in the nineteenth century had a particular meaning and promise for women: self-support. The individual wage raised for women, as it did for men, the possibility of distinguishing oneself from the web of family interdependence; for women especially, because they had behind them the cultural expectation of being 'provided for,' rather than being 'providers,' it raised the vision of escaping economic dependence. I say the 'vision' intentionally, for the wages paid to women were not, on the whole, such as to allow them economic independence – not even a living for one, by and large, much less one plus dependants – but enough to enable them to contribute along with other wage-earners to family maintenance. For women, the link between economic self-support and personal autonomy was forged with greater and more repeated struggle than was the case with men, because of women's limited earnings and their persistent obligations (and hence self-images) as unpaid daughters, wives and mothers. Nevertheless the earning of wages by women had to have, conceptually and over the long term, a profoundly individualizing tendency, wearing away at the assumption and the reality that woman obtained her sustenance and support and gave her services within the family circle.

It is on this mental universe of working women's potentially conflicting loyalties and self-concepts that Sarah Eisenstein's work focused. Her study of working women's consciousness at the turn of the century, so definitely rooted in the published sources of the period, and so fruitfully drawing on the well of feminist thinking about consciousness, and its Marxian underground stream, was unique for its time. Most of what current writers rely on to describe women's labor history has been published since the mid-1970s and did not enter Sarah Eisenstein's research; she had a vision of her own, arising out of an impasse in social theory and capable of generating not only new theoretical but new substantive advances. She developed her approach before Tamara Hareven published her work on the intersection of 'family time and industrial time,' before Joan Scott and Louise Tilly addressed working women's move from household to factory, before the appearance of Herbert Gutman's book *Work, Culture and Society in Industrializing America*, Alice Kessler-Harris's articles on organized women or recent survey of wage-earning women's history, or much public airing of Marxist-feminist ideas on the intersection of capitalism and patriarchy with women's work.[1]

Attempting to revise social theory so as to deal adequately with women workers both as workers and as women, Eisenstein brought to the examination of the late nineteenth and early twentieth century her understanding that family relations and expectations for women could not be considered separate from their experience of wage work. She was searching for a conceptualization of working women's consciousness that would recognize the demands and loyalties of both family and work, would place adequate emphasis on both ideology and behavior, and would acknowledge the impact of both previous cultural traditions and the force of new circumstances. All of these propositions stemmed from her central concern to establish a theoretical formulation which would admit the operation in working women's lives of the dominant bourgeois ideology of gender spheres without either sacrificing or idealizing the integrity of working women's point of view.

Eisenstein's exploration of late Victorian ideas regarding women and work took an especially innovative tack. Her analysis of advice books written to girls and women entering the labor market is a *tour de force*. Recognizing that this literature, by and large, was not addressed to the ordinary female wage-earner who was her main subject, Eisenstein used it nevertheless to illuminate the ideological structures which fatefully conditioned the ordinary wage-earner's view of herself. More than one other book has attempted a history of ideas of success, entrepreneurship, or the work ethic in America, but in them Horatio Alger is always a man.[2] Eisenstein, in contrast, tantalizingly indicated the usefulness of analysing by gender in this (as in every other) area. She found incentives and encouragements towards promotion reiterated in the prescriptive literature, despite the fact that women's jobs were so largely dead-end; she found constant distinctions and levels of status drawn among workers, and the assumption that success for the one meant 'the others' remaining below; she found a pervasive link between the status of any work and the perceived 'character' – that nineteenth-century ruling idea – of those who do it. How far these assumptions were ones carried over from the literature of success for males, how far they owed to shifting class relations in America, how far they uniquely indicated women's situation, and why, are fascinating questions raised by Eisenstein's study.

Eisenstein detailed the identification of 'womanhood' with

'ladyhood' in nineteenth-century ideology, building on Gerda Lerner's stimulating article 'The Lady and the Mill Girl,'[3] and argued that wage-earning women were thus by definition excluded from womanly respectability. Moreover, she suggested that this exclusion rested on an ideological separation of work from home life, of public from private arena, which represented accurately neither the material world nor working women's perception of it. Her incipient critique anticipated the work of Elizabeth Pleck, Joan Kelly, Michele Rosaldo, and other feminist scholars who in the late 1970s began to articulate the defects inherent in accepting, even for analytic purposes, the separation of life into 'spheres' of public/private, production/reproduction, male/female.[4] Eisenstein warned, for instance, not to overestimate working girls' experience of the conflict between work and home; she proposed that 'working outside the home presented a way of fulfilling old commitments in new circumstances' before such historians as Thomas Dublin or Joan Scott and Louise Tilly had come to similar conclusions.[5] Eisenstein's identification of cameraderie at work as a central element in working women's self-definition, and her examination of working girls' views of marriage and romantic love, also presaged themes of Leslie Woodcock Tentler's, building on similar sources and often showing more adeptness at piercing through middle-class observers' characterizations of working-class attitudes.[6]

If feminist historians' pursuit of women's consciousness in history has sometimes adopted the Marxist concept of class consciousness wholesale, proposing a 'gender consciousness' that is the same for all women, Eisenstein's work disabuses us of that notion, and begins instead a conceptualization that would include class and gender. She lays the theoretical groundwork for conceptualization of working-class women's self-discovery as a social class. Middle and upper-middle class women presumably 'discovered' their character as a class – thus allowing the women's rights movement to develop – because they believed they shared the womanly characteristics of domesticity, morality, nurturance and gentility, and because (as Eisenstein points out) in evangelical reform and other voluntary associations they were able to act collectively. Influenced by, and for the most part accepting the same defi-

nition of womanhood, working-class women were none the less
outside of (both excluded from and not willing to join) that
collectivity because of its aspect of gentility – its conflation of
'womanhood' with 'ladyhood.' The shared experience of wage-
work, and even more profoundly, the shared experience of the
conflicts (ideological, perceived, actual) between wage-work
and domestic life, Eisenstein suggests, gave working-class
women a slightly different but no less coherent perspective
from which to perceive their common interests, their identification as a class. (It is striking, and congruent with Eisenstein's thinking, that when middle-class female orators from
the mid-nineteenth through the early twentieth century
addressed their 'sisters,' they imagined they addressed all
women, whom they assumed shared their own characteristics;
whereas wage-earning women orators of the same era who
spoke of their 'sisters' meant wage-earning women, whom they
understood had characteristics and outlooks distinct from
those of more prosperous women.) It is a great loss that Eisenstein herself will not fulfil the brilliant promise of her early
work. Others, perhaps, following her lead, may bring it to
fruition.

Notes

1 Introduction

1 Teachers' College Library, Columbia University; the University of Minnesota; and University of Illinois at Chicago Circle.

2 Tamiment Library, New York University; University of Illinois at Chicago Circle; and the Library of Congress.

3 Schlesinger Library, Radcliffe College; The Chicago Historical Society; and Tamiment Library, New York University.

4 Wisconsin Historical Society, Newberry Library, Chicago, and Rose Pastor Stokes Papers, Yale University; and Wayne State University Labor History Archives.

5 Women of these backgrounds were strongly represented in the garment industry of eastern and midwestern cities, the focal point of trade union campaigns among women in the early twentieth century. Women of many other nationalities were employed in textile, boot and shoe, food processing, paper products and a variety of additional manufacturing industries.

6 Jane Humphries, 'The Working Class Family, Women's Liberation, and Class Struggle: The Case of Nineteenth Century British History,' *Review of Radical Political Economics*, vol. 9, no. 3, 1977, pp. 25–41, and 'Class Struggle and the Persistence of the Working Class Family,' *Cambridge Journal of Economics*, vol. 1, 1977, pp. 241–58; and Louise A. Tilly and Joan W. Scott, *Women, Work and Family*, New York, Holt, Rinehart & Winston, 1978.

7 Herbert Gutman, *Work, Culture and Society in Industrializing America*, New York, Alfred A. Knopf, 1976; Virginia Yans-McLaughlin, *Family and Community. Italian Immigrants in Buffalo, 1880–1930*, Ithaca, NY, Cornell University Press, 1977.

8 See Theresa M. McBride, *The Domestic Revolution. The Modernisation of Household Service in England and France 1820–1920*, New York, Holmes & Meier, 1976, and Patricia Branca, *Women in Europe since 1750*, New York, St Martin's

Press, 1978, ch. 2 and epilogue, for discussions of change in women's work from a modernization perspective.

9 Nancy Schrom Dye, 'Creating a Feminist Alliance: Sisterhood and Class Conflict in the New York Women's Trade Union League, 1903–1914,' *Feminist Studies*, vol. 2, no. 2/3, 1975, pp. 24–38; and Robin Miller Jacoby, 'The Women's Trade Union League and American Feminism,' *Feminist Studies*, vol. 3, no. 1/ 2, 1975, pp. 126–40.

2 Bread and roses: working women's consciousness, 1905– 1920

1 See John Horton's discussion of transcendent and immanent approaches to social analysis in his article, 'Order and Conflict Theories of Social Problems as Competing Ideologies,' *American Journal of Sociology*, vol. 71, no. 5., 1966 pp. 701–13.

2 Louis Levine, *The Women's Garment Workers*, New York, B. W. Huebsch, 1924, pp. 84 and 114.

3 US Census for 1910, cited by Alice Henry in *The Trade Union Woman*, New York and London, D. Appleton & Co., 1915; p. 186; also Robert Smuts, *Women and Work in America*, New York, Columbia University Press, 1959, p. 18.

4 Eleanor Flexner, *Century of Struggle*, Cambridge, MA, Harvard University Press, 1959, chs 3, 9, 14 and 18.

5 Levine, op. cit.

6 Cf. Smuts, op. cit., and Flexner, op. cit.

7 Jesse Lemisch, 'Towards a Democratic History,' Ann Arbor, MI, Radical Education Project publication.

8 Agnes Nestor describes encounters with such women at legislative hearings in her autobiography, *Woman's Labor Leader*, Rockford, IL, Bellevue Books, 1954.

9 Henry, op. cit., pp. 186 and 191.

10 Levine, op. cit., p. 145.

11 Elizabeth Butler, *Saleswomen in Mercantile Stores*, New York, Russell Sage Foundation, 1913, pp. 72 and 75.

12 Ibid., pp. 117 and 119.

13 Rose Schneiderman in a letter in *Life and Labor*, May 1920, p. 153.

14 The study was cited in Smuts, op. cit., p. 51.

15 Butler, op. cit., p. 121.

16 Lillian Matthews, *Women in Trade Unions in San Francisco*, Berkeley, University of California Press, 1913, pp. 2 and 3.

17 Annie Marion MacLean, *The Wage-Earning Woman*, New York, Macmillan, 1910, p. 98. She is commenting on cities in the mid-west.

18 Mary H. Jones, *Autobiography of Mother Jones*, Chicago, Charles H. Kerr & Co., 1925, p. 237.

19 Schneiderman, op. cit., p. 153.

20 Quoted in an article on 'Organization and the Southern Woman,' *Life and Labor*, June 1920, p. 163.
21 Anonymous, *Four Years in the Underbrush*, New York, C. Scribner's Sons, 1921, p. 310. The author is citing remarks made to her by women with whom she worked.
22 Quoted by Carola Woerishoeffer in her report on conditions in New York laundries, in Henry, op. cit., p. 196.
23 Ibid., p. 34.
24 Cf., for instance, the report of Anna Willard's marriage in *Life and Labor*, vol. 12, p. 30. She had been president of the Chicago Waitresses Union for five years, but gave up the post when she married. Both her marriage and election of a new president are reported in the same article with no explanation considered necessary.
25 Rose Schneiderman with Lucy Goldthwaite, *All For One*, New York, Paul S. Eriksson, 1967, p. 50.
26 Jones, op. cit., p. 239.
27 *Life and Labor*, July 1912, p. 216. See also Agnes Nestor, *Life and Labor*, April 1912, p. 138.
28 Schneiderman letter, op. cit.
29 *Life and Labor*, July 1912, p. 215.
30 Ibid., June 1912, pp. 190–91.
31 Ibid., June 1912, pp. 216–17.
32 Ibid., June 1920, p. 164.
33 Matthews, op. cit., pp. 2 and 3.
34 Mollie Schepps' speech, *Life and Labor*, July 1912, pp. 215–16.
35 Elizabeth Dutcher, 'The Triangle Fire,' in *Life and Labor*, August 1911, p. 265.
36 *New York Sun*, 14 November 1863, 'Working Women.'
37 Dutcher, op. cit., p. 265. See also the report by the New England Civic Federation on women in relief workrooms.
38 *Life and Labor*, December 1911, p. 384.
39 Ibid., September 1911, p. 259, editorial.
40 Levine, op. cit., p. 54.
41 Mabel Taylor, 'Where the Men are to Blame,' *Life and Labor*, June 1921.
42 *Life and Labor*, January 1912, p. 31, neckwear workers' organization.
43 Ibid., January 1918, p. 58.
44 Schneiderman letter, op. cit.
45 Henry, op. cit., discusses this subject in the first four chapters.
46 *Life and Labor*, July 1912, p. 215. From the speech given by Maggie Hinchey, a laundry worker, at the Cooper Union meeting.
47 See also *Life and Labor*, April 1911, p. 126, and August 1912, p. 210.
48 Smuts, op. cit., pp. 88–9.
49 *Life and Labor*, August 1912, p. 228.

50 Sue Ainslie Clark and Edith Wyatt, *Making Both Ends Meet*, New York, Macmillan, 1911, pp. 28–9, and Anon., *Four Years*, p. 28.
51 Clark and Wyatt, op. cit., p. 29; quote from a salesgirl.
52 Consumer's League of New York, *Behind the Scenes in a Restaurant*, New York, 1916, p. 36; quote from a waitress.
53 Smuts, op. cit., pp. 88–9.
54 Henry, op. cit., p. 132.
55 *Life and Labor*, July 1911, p. 195.
56 Ibid., April 1912, p. 99.
57 Nestor, op. cit., p. 117.
58 Schneiderman, *All for One*, p. 86.
59 Nestor, op. cit., p. 117.
60 Levine, op. cit., p. 158, quoting William Mailly writing in the *Independent* about the shirtwaist makers' strike.
61 Clark and Wyatt, op. cit., p. 151.
62 *Life and Labor*, February 1912, p. 55.
63 Matthews, op. cit., p. 70.
64 *Life and Labor*, December 1911, p. 384.
65 Ibid., April 1912, p. 99.
66 Ibid., August 1912, p. 288; report on a speech on suffrage delivered by Rose Schneiderman to a group of wealthy women.

3 The study of working women's consciousness

1 Max Weber, 'Class, Status, Party', in *From Max Weber*, ed. H. H. Gerth and C. Wright Mills, New York, Oxford University Press, 1958, p. 184.
2 Karl Mannheim, 'On the Nature of Economic Ambition and its Significance for the Social Education of Man,' in *Essays on the Sociology of Knowledge*, London, Routledge & Kegan Paul, 1952, note p. 236.
3 Eric Hobsbawm, 'Class Consciousness in History,' in *Aspects of History and Class Consciousness*, ed. István Mészaros, London, Routledge & Kegan Paul for the Merlin Book Club, 1971, pp. 7–8.
4 Karl Mannheim, 'The Problem of the Intelligentsia,' in *Essays on the Sociology of Culture*, London, Routledge & Kegan Paul, 1956, p. 96. Also cf. 'On the Problem of Generations' in *Essays on the Sociology of Knowledge*.
5 Karl Marx and Frederick Engels, 'The German Ideology', in *Writings of the Young Marx on Philosophy and Society*, ed. Lloyd D. Easton and Kurt H. Guddat, Garden City, NY, Anchor Books, 1967, p. 456.
6 Robert Michels, 'The Origins of the Anti-Capitalist Mass Spirit,' trans. Kurt Shell, in *Man in Contemporary Society: A Sourcebook*, vol. I, ed. Contemporary Civilization Staff,

Columbia College, New York, Columbia University Press, 1955, pp. 740–65.

7 Karl Korsch, *Karl Marx*, London, Chapman & Hall, 1938; reprint edn, New York, Russell & Russell, 1963, p. 193.

8 See, for the first argument, Aileen Kraditor, *Ideas of the Woman Suffrage Movement, 1890–1920*, New York, Columbia University Press, 1965, and Eleanor Flexner, *Century of Struggle*, Cambridge, MA, Harvard University Press, 1959; on the second, William O'Neill, *Everyone Was Brave*, Chicago, Quadrangle Books, 1969; on the fourth, O'Neill, 'The Victorians taught women to think of themselves as a social class,' in ibid., p. 6; on the last, Alice Rossi's argument in 'Social Roots of the Woman's Movement in America,' the Introduction to part 2 of her *The Feminist Papers*, New York, Bantam, 1973.

9 Ibid., pp. 265 ff.

10 Barbara Welter, 'The Cult of True Womanhood,' *American Quarterly*, vol. 18, no. 2, 1966, pp. 151–74.

11 Mannheim, 'Intelligentsia,' p. 96.

12 This is evident in almost any biography or autobiography of the early feminists. Cf., for example, Elizabeth Cady Stanton's autobiography, *Eighty Years and More* (New York, T. Fisher Unwin, 1898; reprint edn, New York, Schocken Books, 1971) or Gerda Lerner, *The Grimke Sisters from South Carolina*, New York, Schocken Books, 1969.

13 Alice Rossi describes this process: 'women continued to form women's auxiliaries to local abolition societies and corresponded with each other about their work. By 1837 there was a national system of female societies to support the petition campaigns. Critical to this experience was the fact that in their cause women brought to bear house-to-house agitation and hence face-to-face influence in their own neighborhoods. . . . It was in the abolition movement of the 1830's, therefore, that American women first showed some corporate expression of their political will, and it was from this movement that the women's rights leaders acquired the ideas about political organization which they applied to their own cause in the late 1840's' (op. cit., p. 263).

14 Cf. Richard Hoggart, *The Uses of Literacy*, Boston, Beacon Press, 1961, and Herbert Gans, *The Urban Villagers*, New York, The Free Press, 1962, for example.

15 Hobsbawm, op. cit., p. 9.

16 E. P. Thompson, 'Time, Work-Discipline, and Industrial Capitalism,' *Past and Present*, no. 38, 1967, p. 79.

17 Mannheim, 'Intelligentsia,' pp. 99–100.

18 Margaret Benston, for one, does make this argument in her article 'The Political Economy of Women's Liberation,' *Monthly Review*, vol. 21, no. 4, 1969, pp. 13–27.

19 'Every social system, even a total society, has a paramount

value pattern' (Talcott Parsons, 'An Approach to the Sociology of Knowledge,' in *The Sociology of Knowledge*, ed. James E. Curtis and John W. Petras, New York and Washington, Praeger, 1970, p. 284).

20 It may be noted that this approach informs much of modern sociological discussion of the importance of work in women's lives. The form it takes in Parsons's own work is to view the experience of women workers as an example of the tension generated by conflicting role requirements. See, for example, 'Age and Sex in the Social Structure of the U.S.,' in his *Essays in Sociological Theory*, rev. edn, Chicago, The Free Press, 1954. Another version, which sees it as an example of individual adjustment of values and expectations in response to changing circumstances, is not essentially different theoretically. This is exemplified in the work of Lotte Bailyn, 'Notes on the Role of Choice in the Psychology of Professional Women,' in *Women in America*, ed. Robert Lifton, Boston, Beacon Press, 1964, and Mirra Komarovsky, *Blue Collar Marriage*, New York, Vintage Books, 1967. Alice Rossi discusses this point in her article 'Equality between the Sexes' in the Lifton volume.

21 Cf. *Ideology and Utopia*, New York and London, Harcourt, Brace, Jovanovich, 1936, and 'Competition as a Cultural Phenomenon' in Mannheim, *Essays on the Sociology of Knowledge*.

22 Walter Miller, 'Lower Class Culture as a Generating Milieu of Gang Delinquency,' *Journal of Social Issues*, vol. 14, no. 3, 1958, pp. 5–19; Herbert Hyman, 'The Value Systems of Different Classes' in *Class, Status and Power*, ed. R. Bendix and S. M. Lipset, 2nd edn, New York, The Free Press, 1966; Gans, op. cit., ch. 11; Maurice Halbwachs, *The Psychology of Social Class*, London, Heinemann, 1958.

23 E. P. Thompson, *The Making of the English Working Class*, New York, Vintage, 1963, p. 177.

24 Parsons himself points to the necessity of articulating value-statements with empirical standards or definitions 'at the highest level.' Cf. 'Sociology of Knowledge,' pp. 285 ff.

25 Mannheim, for example, argues the point: 'Sociological analysis shows that this public interpretation of reality is not simply 'there;' nor, on the other hand, is it the result of a 'systematic thinking out;' it is the stake for which men fight. . . . Different interpretations of the world for the most part correspond to the particular positions the groups occupy in their struggle for power' ('Competition,' p. 199).

26 Parkin, *Class Inequality and Political Order*, New York and Washington, Praeger, 1971, p. 82. Both E. P. Thompson and Reinhard Bendix demonstrate these points, although from very different perspectives, in their respective discussions of the genesis and establishment of values 'appropriate' to

industrialized societies. In the work of both, the generalization of values and attitudes about work, time, and discipline appears not as an automatic reflection of the process of industrialization, but as the result of active, directed efforts to establish them on the part of the groups whose interests they served. Cf. Thompson, 'Time, Work-Discipline, . . .' and Bendix, *Work and Authority in Modern Industry*, New York, Harper & Row, 1963.

27 See, for example, Herbert Marcuse's argument in *One-Dimensional Man*, Boston, Beacon Press, 1964.

28 Parkin, op. cit., p. 92.

29 Ibid., p. 95.

30 In this regard, his argument resembles Richard Hamilton's in *Affluence and the French Worker in the Fourth Republic* (Princeton, NJ, Princeton University Press, 1967), who also emphasizes the centrality of exposure to party ideology as a factor in working-class radicalism.

31 These individual misfortunes were in fact a widespread social phenomenon in the nineteenth century, representing to some degree the costs and disruptions of industrial growth and the absence of social welfare institutions to cope with them. See, for examples, Robert W. Smuts, *Women and Work in America*, New York, Columbia University Press, 1959, ch. 2. To some extent, of course, the New England mill towns of the early part of the century, e.g. Lowell, represent a different case, in some ways closer to the group we are studying.

32 See Welter, op. cit., pp. 167–8, and, particularly on the generalization of the standards of ladylike behavior, Gerda Lerner, 'The Lady and the Mill Girl: Changes in the Status of Women in the Age of Jackson,' *Midcontinent American Studies Journal*, vol. 10, no. 1, 1969, pp. 5–15.

33 On these developments, see Page Smith, *Daughters of the Promised Land*, Boston, Little, Brown, 1970; Duncan Crow, *The Victorian Woman*, New York, Stein & Day, 1972, especially pp. 352ff.; Martha Vicinus' Introduction to her *Suffer and Be Still*, Bloomington, IN, Indiana University Press, 1973; Peter Cominus, 'Innocent Femina Sensualis in Unconscious Conflict,' in Vicinus, pp. 171–2, 166; and Flexner and O'Neill, op. cit. For contemporary recognition of the growth of women's employment, see, for example, Azel Ames, *Sex in Industry*, Boston, J. R. Osgood & Co., 1875, Jaspar Earle, *The Real Trouble and the Way Out*, Kansas City, MO, n.p., 1897; the Rev. Nehemiah Boynton, 'Working Girls,' in *The Arena*, vol. 2, no. 9, August 1890.

34 Smuts, op. cit., ch. 2.

35 Some of this work was presented at the Second Berkshire Conference on the History of Women, held at Radcliffe College on 25–7 October 1974. It included papers by Margery Davies, 'The Feminization of White-Collar Occupations,' Judith Smith,

'The "New Woman" Knows How to Type: Some Connections between Sexual Ideology and Clerical Work, 1890–1930,' and Elyce Rotella, 'Occupational Segregation: A Case Study of American Clerical Workers, 1870–1930.'

36 This tendency is evident in Tamara Hareven's work on Manchester, NH, including the paper she delivered at the Second Berkshire Conference, 'Women's Time, Family Time and Industrial Time: An Analysis of the Relationship of Work Careers and Family Conditions of Women Workers . . . 1910– 1940,' the paper delivered at the same Conference by Joan Scott and Louise Tilly, 'Daughters, Wives, Mothers, Workers: Peasants and Working Class Women in the Transition to an Industrial Economy in France,' and in articles such as Daniel Walkowitz, 'Working-Class Women in the Gilded Age: Factory, Community and Family Life Among Cohoes, New York, Cotton Workers,' *Journal of Social History*, vol. 5, no. 4, 1972, pp. 464– 90, and Virginia Yans-McLaughlin, 'Patterns of Work and Family Organization: Buffalo's Italians,' *The Journal of Interdisciplinary History*, vol. 2, no. 2, 1971, pp. 299–314.

37 For reasons to be more fully developed in the study itself, we will also include women who worked in certain service trades, such as laundries, and in retail sales, because of the degree of similarity to factory work in the recruitment patterns for workers in these fields, and the consequent similarity in the characteristics of the workers attracted to them, and because they involved similar contrasts in terms of the conditions of work to the dominant images of womanhood.

38 Stearns, 'Working-Class Women in Britain, 1890–1914,' in Vicinus, op. cit., p. 112.

4 Victorian ideology and working women

1 The following discussion is necessarily summary in nature. I have drawn on discussions of Victorian ideology and attitudes in general works on women in the period as well as those which deal specifically with working women. Among these are Page Smith, *Daughters of the Promised Land*, Boston, Little, Brown, 1970; Duncan Crow, *The Victorian Woman*, New York, Stein & Day, 1972; Arthur W. Calhoun, *A Social History of the American Family*, 3 vols, Cleveland, Arthur H. Clark, 1917–19; Eleanor Flexner, *Century of Struggle*, Cambridge, MA, Harvard University Press, 1959; Andrew Sinclair, *The Emancipation of the American Woman*, New York, Harper & Row, 1966; Robert Smuts, *Women and Work in America*, New York, Columbia University Press, 1959; Wanda Neff, *Victorian Working Women*, London, Allen & Unwin, 1929; Martha Vicinus, ed., *Suffer and Be Still*, Bloomington, IN, Indiana University Press, 1973; and Nancy Cott's introduction to her collection, *Root of Bitterness*,

New York, E. P. Dutton, 1972. In some cases I have used richer material which deals with England to supplement sources on the United States. The two most important studies of ideology about women in the United States during the Victorian period are Barbara Welter, 'The Cult of True Womanhood,' *American Quarterly*, vol. 18, no. 2, 1966, pp. 151–74, on which I draw heavily in this chapter, and Gerda, Lerner, 'The Lady and the Mill Girl: Changes in the Status of Women in the Age of Jackson,' *Midcontinent American Studies Journal*, vol. 10, no. 1, 1969, pp. 5–15.

2 Welter, op. cit., p. 62.

3 George Burnap, *Sphere and Duties of Woman*, cited in Welter, op. cit., p. 170.

4 Mrs Sigourney, *Letters to Mothers*, cited in Welter, op. cit., p. 171.

5 Mrs Emma C. Embury, 'Female Education,' *Ladies' Companion*, VIII, January 1838, cited in Welter, op. cit., p. 172.

6 Rev. J. N. Danforth, 'Maternal Relations,' *The Ladies' Casket*, N.Y. 1850?, cited in Welter, op. cit., p. 171.

7 Dr William Acton, cited in Steven Marcus, *The Other Victorians*, New York, Vintage, 1964, p. 31.

8 Ibid., p. 31.

9 Vicinus, op. cit., p. ix.

10 Welter, op. cit., p. 158.

11 Vicinus, op. cit., p. x.

12 M. Jeanne Petersen, 'The Victorian Governess: Status Incongruence in Family and Society,' in Vicinus, op. cit.

13 Alexis de Tocqueville, *Democracy in America*, vol. 2, New York, Random House, 1945, p. 201.

14 Crow, op. cit., p. 29. His discussion of prudery in England, pp. 23–6, and the US, pp. 27ff and 63 is particularly interesting.

15 Welter, op. cit., pp. 167–8.

16 T. S. Arthur, 'Sweethearts and Wives,' *Godey's Ladies Book*, December 1841, reprinted in *Root of Bitterness*, ed. Nancy Cott, New York, E. P. Dutton, 1972, pp. 157–70.

17 Ibid., p. 170.

18 Alice Clark's *Working Life of Women in the Seventeenth Century*, London, G. Routledge & Sons, 1919, reprint edn, New York, Augustus Kelley, 1967, describes both the range of women's work in medieval England and effects of capitalist development on narrowing and restricting it. See also Ivy Pinchbeck, *Women Workers and the Industrial Revolution 1750–1850*, London, Routledge & Kegan Paul, 1930, reprint edn, New York, Augustus Kelley, 1969.

19 See Philippe Ariès, *Centuries of Childhood*, New York, Alfred A. Knopf, 1962, Part III, Sect. 2.

20 See Calhoun, op. cit., vol. I; Smith, op. cit., chs 3 and 4; Edith Abbott, *Women in Industry*, New York and London, D. Appleton

& Co., 1910, reprint edn, New York, Source Book Press, 1970, ch. 2; Smuts, op. cit.

21   Ibid., p. 56.

22   Ibid., p. 57.

23   Ibid., chs 3 and 4; Hannah Josephson, *The Golden Threads*, New York, Duell, Sloan and Pearce, 1949.

24   Alexander Hamilton, *Report on Manufactures*, cited in Abbott, op. cit., p. 50.

25   Ibid., p. 51.

26   Matthew Carey in public address in 1824 before Philadelphia Society for Promoting Agriculture, cited in ibid., p. 58.

27   See Lerner, op. cit.; Smith, op. cit.; and Calhoun, op. cit., vols. I and II.

28   Smith, op. cit., p. 57.

29   Ibid., p. 59.

30   Cited in Calhoun, op. cit., vol. II, p. 201.

31   Cited in ibid., vol. II, pp. 201–2.

32   See, for example, Lucy Larcom's *A New England Girlhood*, Boston, Houghton Mifflin, 1889, reprint edition, New York, Arno Press, 1974. Larcom, an early mill operative in Lowell, writing about 'Old-World' attitudes toward factory girls, says of American factory girls: 'But they themselves belonged to the New World . . . and they were making their own traditions, to hand down to their Republican descendents, – one of which was and is that honest work has no need to . . . humble itself in a nation like ours' (p. 201).

33   Crow, op. cit., p. 61ff.

34   Lerner, op. cit., p. 11.

35   For background on these developments, see Abbott, op. cit.; Smuts, op. cit.; Smith, op. cit.; and Lerner, op. cit.

36   See Abbott, op. cit. Also, Elizabeth M. Bacon, 'The Growth of Household Conveniences in the United States from 1865–1900,' unpublished PhD Thesis, Radcliffe College, 1942, for a detailed discussion of changes in women's work in the home under the impact of industrialization throughout the nineteenth century. Meta Stern Lilenthal, *From Fireside to Factory*, New York, Rand School, 1916, is an interesting popular presentation of this argument, as well as an example of the ways in which feminists made use of the image of women's earlier productive activity.

37   William O'Neill makes this point in *Everyone Was Brave*, Chicago, Quadrangle, 1969, pp. 3–7. He argues, following Aries, 'that the conjugal family was a recent development,' which placed new burdens on Victorian women; 'In completing the transformation of the family . . . into a strictly defined nuclear unit at the very center of social life, the Victorians laid a burden on women which many of them could or would not bear' (p. 4). The Victorians attempted to compensate women for these burdens with the mystique of true womanhood and the cult of

the home, 'Hence the endless polemics on the moral purity and spiritual genius of woman which found their highest expression in the home, but which had to be safeguarded at all costs from the corrupting effects of the man-made world beyond the domestic circle' (p. 5). O'Neill argues further that the feminist movement can be seen as a form of resistance to this recent encroachment on broader, and remembered, female roles, and to the ideological developments which accompanied it.

38 Mary Ryan, 'American Society and the Cult of Domesticity, 1830–1860,' Unpublished PhD Thesis, University of California at Santa Barbara, 1971.

39 Welter, op. cit., p. 151.

40 Ibid., p. 152. See also Vicinus, op. cit., p. xii; Eva Figes, *Patriarchal Attitudes*, New York, Stein & Day, 1970, p. 110.

41 Charles W. Marsh, *Recollections, 1837–1910*, Chicago, 1910, cited in Smuts, op. cit., p. 6.

42 See Crow, op. cit., pp. 23–6; 30ff; 45–57; Petersen, op. cit., pp. 10–12, Vicinus, op. cit., introduction; Figes, op. cit., pp. 37, 85, 70; Smith, op. cit., chs 3, 4, 5, 14; Calhoun, op. cit., vol. II, chs 6 and 10; Lerner, op. cit., and Neff, op. cit., ch. 6. Steven Marcus suggests an additional connection between Victorian ideology and the tensions of this period in the development of capitalism. He points to the parallel between Victorian views of sexuality – male as well as female – and their reaction to the uncertainties of economic life: 'The fantasies . . . here have to do with economics; the body is regarded as a productive system with only a limited amount of material at its disposal. And the model on which the notion of semen is formed is clearly that of money . . . up until the end of the nineteenth century the chief English colloquial expression for the orgasm was "to spend" ' (op. cit., p. 22).

43 James Stirling, *Letters from the Slave States*, London, 1857, cited in Smith, op. cit., p. 90.

44 Calhoun, op. cit., vol. II, p. 229ff.

45 Mrs A. J. Graves, *Woman in America*, New York, 1855, cited in ibid., vol. II, p. 225.

46 See Crow, op. cit.; Flexner, op. cit.; Welter, op. cit.; and Lerner, op. cit.

47 The designation of certain behavior or occupations as 'unwomanly' or 'unnatural' for women was not completely new, of course; the arguments in Anne Hutchinson's trial in the seventeenth century are only one example of the earlier use of such arguments (Flexner, ch. 1). But for the most part, women in the seventeenth and eighteenth century seem to have been criticized more in terms like 'shrewish' or 'sinful' as bad *types* of women, but women none the less. Page Smith argues that 'It was not until the end of the colonial era that the idea of a "suitable" or "proper" sphere of feminine activities began to

emerge. . . . There were, in the early years, very few negative definitions – that this or that activity was unsuitable or inappropriate for a woman to engage in' (op. cit., p. 54). In the early nineteenth century, the idea of 'natural' and 'unnatural' woman gained in importance and currency as a basis of censure; it became possible to be female and not yet truly womanly. In part, of course, this was only a specific form of the more general importance of Nature and Natural Order as a basis of legitimation which emerged as part of the Enlightenment. But it also reflected, I think, the narrowing of roles and behavior for women, and the need for an intensive ideological reinforcement of that development.

48 Neff, op. cit., p. 12.
49 Ibid., p. 37.
50 Ibid., pp. 85–6.
51 Ibid., pp. 147–9.
52 Ibid., p. 164.
53 Ibid., p. 182; Petersen, op. cit.
54 See Crow, op. cit., p. 352ff; Peter Cominus, 'Innocent Femina Sensualis in Unconscious Conflict,' in Vicinus, op. cit., pp. 171–2; Vicinus, op. cit., Introduction, p. xiv; Flexner, op. cit.; O'Neill, op. cit.; Smith, op. cit.
55 Alice H. Rhine, 'Woman in Industry,' in *Woman's Work in America*, ed. Annie Nathan Meyer, New York, Henry Holt & Co., 1891, reprint edn, New York, Arno Press 1972, pp. 286–7.
56 See, for example, Azel Ames, *Sex in Industry*, Boston, J. R. Osgood & Co., 1875, for warnings on the dangers to female biology in work outside the home; Jaspar Earle, *The Real Trouble and the Way Out*, Kansas City, MO, n.p., 1897, for warnings that women are forcing men out of the labor force; The Rev. Nehemiah Boynton, 'Working Girls,' in *The Arena*, vol. II, no. 9, August 1890, calling attention to the 'problem.'
57 *Reports of Cases Argued and Determined in the Supreme Court of the State of Wisconsin*, XXXIX Chicago, 1876, cited in Smuts, op. cit., p. 110.
58 Ella Rodman Church, *Money-Making for Ladies*, New York, Harper & Bros., 1882.
59 Ruth Ashmore, *The Business Girl: In Every Phase of Her Life*, Philadelphia, Ladies Home Journal Library, 1895, pp. 96, 97, 98.
60 Grace H. Dodge; Thomas Hunter; Mrs Mary J. Lincoln; S. S. Packard; Mrs A. M. Palmer, Helen M. Winslow and others, *What Women Can Earn: Occupations of Women and their Compensation*, New York, Frederick A. Stokes, 1898.
61 Helen Churchill Candee, *How Women May Earn a Living*, New York, Macmillan, 1900.
62 Mary A. Laselle and Katherine E. Wiley, *Vocations for Girls*,

Boston, New York, Chicago, Houghton Mifflin, 1913; E. W. Weaver, *Profitable Vocations for Girls*, New York and Chicago, A. S. Barnes Co., 1916; and Helen C. Hoerle and Florence B. Saltzberg, *The Girl and the Job*, New York, Henry Holt & Co., 1919.

63 *Far and Near*, published under the direction of the Auxiliary Society of the Association of Working Girls' Societies of New York; ed. Maria Bowen Chapin; vol. I, November 1890–October 1891; vol. II, November 1891–October 1892; vol. III, November 1892–October 1893.
64 Church, op. cit., pp. 3, 5.
65 Ashmore, op. cit., p. 19.
66 Church, op. cit., p. 5.
67 Candee, op. cit., p. 1.
68 Ibid., p. 10.
69 Dodge *et al.*, op. cit., p. 282.
70 See Weaver, op. cit. and Laselle and Wiley, op. cit.
71 Candee, op. cit., p. 226.
72 Church, op. cit., p. 62.
73 Candee, op. cit., p. 109 – she is discussing a typical annual salary of $600 for a teacher in a private school.
74 Church, op. cit., p. 45 – she is discussing baking and cooking for sale.
75 Laselle and Wiley, op. cit., p. 2.
76 Church, op. cit., p. 77.
77 Ibid., p. 78.
78 Dodge *et al.*, op. cit., p. 120.
79 Church, op. cit., p. 23.
80 See ibid., pp. 21, 26; also Candee, op. cit., and Dodge *et al.*, 1898, op. cit.
81 Church, op. cit., p. 60.
82 Candee, op. cit., p. 157.
83 Ibid., pp. 64–5.
84 See Dodge *et al.*, op. cit.; Weaver, op. cit., for example.
85 Candee, op. cit., p. 169.
86 Ashmore, op. cit., p. 7.
87 Candee, op. cit., p. 120.
88 Ibid., p. 120.
89 Ibid., p. 135.
90 Church, op. cit., p. 185.
91 Ibid., p. 145.
92 Ibid., p. 114.
93 Candee, op. cit., p. 58.
94 Ibid., p. 61.
95 Ibid., p. 93.
96 Ibid., p. 62.
97 Ibid., p. 139.
98 Ibid., pp. 65–6.

99 Ibid., p. 66.
100 Ibid., p. 123.
101 Weaver, op. cit., p. 112.
102 Ibid., p. 28.
103 Ashmore, op. cit., pp. 10, 27.
104 Mary Sanford, 'Typewriting a real Art,' in Dodge *et al.*, op. cit., p. 146.
105 Hoerle and Saltzberg, op. cit., pp. 245–6.
106 Ashmore, op. cit., p. 9.
107 Ibid., p. 89.
108 Ibid., p. 156.
109 Weaver, op. cit., p. 29.
110 Ashmore, op. cit., p. 57.
111 Ibid., p. 58.
112 See ibid., p. 173, and Louise deKoven Bowen, 'The Road to Destruction Made Easy in Chicago,' in *Collected Speeches, Addresses, and Letters of Louise de Koven Bowen*, vol. I, Hull House Archives, University of Illinois at Chicago Circle, for examples.
113 Ruth Ashmore, for example, disliked all 'modern' poetry except Kipling; in addition to his work she recommended Shakespeare, Browning, Tennyson, and 'best of all for girls,' Longfellow, but only 'some' of Shelley and Byron. History was instructive – but not Carlyle, whom she judged 'too bitter.' See Ashmore, op. cit., p. 138ff.
114 Ibid., p. 167.
115 Laselle and Wiley, op. cit., p. 91.
116 Weaver, op. cit., p. 48.
117 Candee, op. cit., pp. 57–8.
118 Ibid., pp. 10–11.
119 Ibid., pp. 11–12.
120 Laselle and Wiley, op. cit., p. 97.
121 Introduction to Dodge *et al.*, op. cit., p. iv.
122 Candee, op. cit., pp. 12–13.
123 Ashmore, op. cit., p. 91.
124 Ibid., p. 86.
125 Ibid., p. 87.
126 Ibid., p. 93.
127 Ibid., p. 153.
128 Ibid., p. 78.
129 Hoerle and Saltzberg, op. cit., p. v.
130 Ibid., p. v.
131 Ibid., Dedication page.
132 Weaver, op. cit., p. 1.
133 Laselle and Wiley, op. cit., p. 3.
134 Ibid., p. iii.
135 It seems likely to me that this shift represented not only changes in attitudes toward women and their increased

participation in the labor force, but also the general development of a more complicated articulation of class structure in this period. With the development of the new industrial rich and the growth of the urbanized middle class after the Civil War, the idea of gentility seems to have shifted from an occupied traditional status to an achieved behavior.

136 Dodge *et al.*, op. cit., p. 276.
137 Ibid., p. 337.
138 Weaver, op. cit., p. 58.
139 See especially ibid.; Laselle and Wiley, op. cit., Hoerle and Saltzberg, op. cit.
140 Weaver, op. cit., p. 59.
141 Laselle and Wiley, op. cit., p. 32.
142 Ibid., p. 34.
143 See, for example, Dorothy Richardson, *The Long Day*, New York, The Century Co., 1905, reprinted in *Women at Work*, ed. William O'Neill, New York, New York Times Books, 1972.
144 Laselle and Wiley, op. cit., p. 39.
145 Weaver, op. cit., p. 63.
146 Ibid., p. 58.
147 See Laselle and Wiley, op. cit., pp. 27–8; Weaver, op. cit., pp. 116–17.
148 Ibid., p. 60.
149 Laselle and Wiley, op. cit., p. 71.
150 Weaver, op. cit., p. 23.
151 Ibid., pp. 88–9.
152 Ibid., p. 23.
153 Laselle and Wiley, op. cit., pp. 7–9.
154 Weaver, op. cit., p. 108; cf. also p. 119.
155 Ibid., p. 110. See also Laselle and Wiley, op. cit., and Hoerle and Saltzberg, op. cit., for similar discussions of factory work.
156 Candee, op. cit., p. 61.
157 Weaver, op. cit., p. 25.
158 Ibid., p. 17.
159 Ibid., p. 31.
160 Quoted in ibid., p. 69.
161 Hoerle and Saltzberg, op. cit., p. 42.
162 Candee, op. cit., pp. 61–2.
163 Weaver, op. cit., p. 29.
164 Laselle and Wiley, op. cit., p. 13.
165 See, for example, Grace Dodge's article in Dodge *et al.*, op. cit., pp. 336, 339; and Laselle and Wiley, op. cit., p. 12.
166 Ibid., p. 31; see also Weaver, op. cit., p. 25.
167 Ashmore, op. cit., p. 30.
168 Hoerle and Saltzberg, op. cit., p. 248.
169 Ashmore, op. cit., pp. 94–5.
170 Ibid., p. 30.

171 Meyer Bloomfield, of The Vocation Bureau, Boston, in his
    Introduction to Laselle and Wiley, op. cit., p. ix.
172 Laselle and Wiley, op. cit., pp. 80–3.
173 Ibid., p. 86.

5 Working women's attitudes toward marriage and work

1 Mary Kingsbury Simkhovitch, 'A New Social Adjustment' in
    *Proceedings of the Academy of Political Science; vol. 1, The
    Economic Position of Women*, New York, The Academy of
    Political Science, Columbia University, 1910, p. 82. Simkhovitch
    was head resident of Greenwich House in New York.
2 Robert A. Woods and Albert J. Kennedy, *Young Working Girls*,
    Boston and New York, Houghton Mifflin, 1913, p. 36. Woods
    and Kennedy were directors of the South End House in Boston;
    the book was prepared for the National Federation of
    Settlements. It was based on questionnaires sent to settlement
    workers and others concerned with working girls across the
    country, and may be taken as a fair representation of the views
    of that group.
3 Ibid., p. 35.
4 See Azel Ames, *Sex in Industry*, Boston, J. R. Osgood & Co.,
    1875, pp. 28–31, for the medical version of this argument, i.e.
    that physical injury to young girls resulted from their working
    during and right after puberty.
5 Woods and Kennedy, op. cit., p. 162.
6 Annie Marion MacLean, *Women Workers and Society*, Chicago,
    A. C. McClurg & Co., 1916, p. 43.
7 Woods and Kennedy, op. cit., p. 163.
8 Ibid., pp. 36–7.
9 The investigators' concern with women 'adrift' emphasizes how
    much women had to be located socially *through* family
    relationships. See Women's Educational and Industrial Union,
    Department of Research, in co-operation with the Massachusetts
    Department of Health, *The Food of Working Women in Boston*,
    Lucille Eaves, director, Boston, Women's Educational and
    Industrial Union, 1917, pp. 68–9, 167–8.
10 MacLean, op. cit., pp. 40–1.
11 Ibid., p. 41.
12 MacLean writes, '[the] effect [of this custom] on the working
    daughters is significant. So long as they remain at home they
    are economically dependent upon their mother and do not learn
    the value of money. When they, in turn, marry . . . they have no
    experience from which to draw, and fall into many errors. They
    heedlessly plunge into buying "on time," that special
    extravagance of wage earners' (p. 41). See also Lillian W. Betts,
    The Leaven in a Great City, New York, Dodd, Mead & Co., 1903,
    pp. 225–31; and Woods and Kennedy, op. cit., pp. 55–7. Often

the same people worried about erosion of the moral authority of parents and wanted to maintain the family as a social and cultural unit, yet could only see wage-earners in classic *laissez-faire* terms. See Richard Hoggart, *The Uses of Literacy*, Boston, Beacon Press, 1961, for a discussion of similar practices in the British working-class family.

13 Lorinda Perry, *Millinery as a Trade for Women*, New York, Longman, 1916, p. 101.

14 Helen Campbell, *Prisoners of Poverty*, Boston, Roberts Brothers, 1887, reprint edn, Westport, CT, Greenwood Press, 1970, p. 71.

15 These patterns of support were documented under tragic circumstances in 1911 for the women killed in the Triangle Shirtwaist Company Fire. The Red Cross distributed funds to the surviving relatives in eighty families. Almost half of the cases involved relatives living abroad who had relied on their daughters' remittances for financial support. They were primarily Jews living in Russia and Eastern Europe. Italian families sent fewer daughters to seek employment in the United States. Leon Stein, *The Triangle Fire*, Philadelphia and New York, J. B. Lippincott, 1962, pp. 131–2.

16 Louis Levine, *The Women's Garment Workers*, New York, B. W. Huebsch, 1924, reprint edition, New York, Arno Press, 1969, pp. 18–20; Rose Cohen, *Out of the Shadow*, New York, George Doran, 1918, pp. 81–4, 89, 108; and Elizabeth Hasanovitz, *One of Them, Chapters from a Passionate Autobiography*, Boston and New York, Houghton Mifflin, 1918, pp. 48–9.

17 Stein, op. cit., pp. 131–2. This pattern characterized the work of Jewish and later Italian women in the garment industry; similar patterns developed for other groups in other industries.

18 Cohen, op. cit., pp. 81–3, 273–6.

19 See Virginia Yans-McLaughlin, 'Patterns of Work and Family Organization: Buffalo's Italians,' *The Journal of Interdisciplinary History*, vol. 2, no. 2, 1971, pp. 299–314, for a discussion of Italian working-class attitudes and practices in Buffalo.

20 See for example, Miss Bertha Scripture (sic), 'Sunday afternoons at the Denison, Students' Club,' in *The Association of Working Girls' Societies*, p. 62, Leonora O'Reilly (LOR) papers, Box 16 Schlesinger Library, Radcliffe College, Cambridge, MA.

21 Italics in original. A 'Second Street Club Member' in *Proceedings of 1st Convention of Working Girls' Societies*, New York, 1890, p. 37.

22 Marie S. Orenstein, 'How the Working Girl of New York City Lives,' in State of New York Factory Investigating Commission, *Fourth Report of the Factory Investigating Commission, 1915*. vol. IV Albany, 1915, pp. 1700–1. Undoubtedly, this report reflects the anxiety of reformers to find women genuinely 'adrift' – of whom there were not as many as they imagined – and

irritation at the degree to which working women made efforts to live with relatives or friends of their families, when they could not live in their parental homes. Still, the phenomenon of women claiming relations with their landladies when in fact there was no basis for it does seem to have been widespread.

23 Louise Marion Bosworth, *The Living Wage of Women Workers*, Philadelphia, The American Academy of Political and Social Science, 1911, p. 31.

24 Ibid., pp. 19–20.

25 *Far and Near*, vol. 1, no. 4, February 1891, p. 61.

26 Ibid., p. 62. Another longer and serialized article on model housekeeping entitled 'Housekeeping for Two' ran in the same year.

27 Bosworth, op. cit., p. 31.

28 Woods and Kennedy, op. cit., p. 39. See also Elizabeth Beardsley Butler, *Women and the Trades*, New York, Russell Sage Foundation, 1911; reprint edn, New York, Arno Press, 1969, p. 373.

29 Woods and Kennedy, op. cit., p. 161.

30 Mrs John Van Vorst and Marie Van Vorst, *The Woman Who Toils. Being the Experiences of Two Gentlewomen as Factory Girls*, New York, Doubleday, Page & Co., 1903, p. 73, describing workers in an upstate New York mill. See also Dorothy Richardson, *The Long Day: The Story of a New York Working Girl*, New York, The Century Co., 1905, reprinted in *Women at Work*, ed. William O'Neill, New York, New York Times Books, 1972.

31 See Richardson, op. cit.; Van Vorst and Van Vorst, op. cit., Anonymous, *Four Years in the Underbrush*, New York, C. Scribner's Sons, 1921, and Sue Ainslie Clark and Edith Wyatt, *Making Both Ends Meet*, New York, Macmillan, 1911. The canons of this literary backwater would make an interesting study in themselves. Although stereotyped and condescending, they are a useful source for some aspects of working women's lives, if used critically. After 1905 or so, they were overshadowed by more objective and scientific studies sponsored by foundations and social service agencies. It is interesting, though, to note the influence of the former occasionally cropping up in the later work.

32 Betts, op. cit., p. 205. Betts's book, written earlier than those described above, was based on her activities as a charity and social worker in New York, particularly with working girls' clubs, not on a stint as a worker, but the citation is archetypical.

33 Van Vorst and Van Vorst, op. cit., p. 132.

34 Ibid., p. 132.

35 B.W.M. on 'Married and Single Life,' in *Thoughts of Busy Girls,*

ed. Grace H. Dodge, New York, Cassell Publishing Co., 1892, pp. 19–20.

36 Ibid., p. 20.

37 Ibid., p. 22.

38 Richardson, op. cit., p. 73. See Helen Waite Papashvily, *All the Happy Endings*, New York, Harper & Row 1956, pp. 190–200, for a description of Laura Jean Libbey.

39 Woods and Kennedy, op. cit., p. 32.

40 Rose Schneiderman with Lucy Goldthwaite, *All For One*, New York, Paul S. Eriksson, 1967, p. 41. Schneiderman also mentioned that later on when she met men in trade union work, she discovered 'that I could fall in love very easily, though unsuccessfully', p. 42.

41 Grace Dodge, Outline of Address to the Girls' Friendly Societies, Brooklyn, NY, 23 January 1890, PWPA Notebook, p. 39, Teachers' College Archives (TC), New York.

42 Grace Dodge, Notes of address to girls' club at Danielsonville, Conn., 26 September 1892. In PWPA Notebook, p. 148, TC.

43 Woods and Kennedy, op. cit., p. 156.

44 Typescript 'Report' of the Conference, 20 January 1916. Social Welfare History Archives (SWHA) n.p. (4 pages). United Neighborhood Houses Collection, File 1. University of Minnesota, Minneapolis.

45 Third National Convention of Working Women's Clubs, Philadelphia, April 1896, p. 147. Leonora O'Reilly Papers, Schlesinger Library, Radcliffe College, Box 13, File 297. Selection is unsigned, identified only by club name: possibly by club 'worker', not a working girl. The working girls also adopted the snooty style of referring to the 'typical working girl.'

46 The annual reports and descriptive brochures of settlements throughout the period reflect the continuing importance of cooking and home-making courses in their programs, although it is difficult to establish the numbers involved with any precision. Cf. for examples, the annual report or newsletters of The Westminster House (Buffalo, NY), Badin Street Settlement (Rochester, NY), College Settlements, Hartley House, Madison House, Henry Street and Union Settlements in New York; Denison House and Norfolk House in Boston, the papers of the National Federation of Settlements at the Social Welfare History Archives, University of Minnesota, or the programs and syllabuses of Hull House in Hull House Scrapbooks, vol. II at Hull House, University of Illinois at Chicago Circle. Also, see Allen F. Davis, *Spearheads for Reform*, New York, Oxford University Press, 1967, pp. 45–6. Usually these were either straight classes in housekeeping or regular programs forming part of the plan of general Girls' Clubs. One's attention is caught, however, by occasional poignant combination with other interests, as in the 'Home Making and Literary Club' of twenty-

three young women listed in the Neighborhood House Program, January 1902. National Federation of Settlements Collection SWHA.

47 M. J. on 'Married and Single Life,' in Dodge, ed., *Thoughts of Busy Girls*, p. 18. This was certainly the case with girls in the Working Girls' Clubs. It is somewhat harder to establish the direct influence of ideas in settlement clubs, since the available records do not include examples of what the girls themselves thought. Yet the settlements are probably the more important instance, since they affected wider numbers of girls, both directly in their own clubs, and in their indirect influence on public school curricula. We can be sure, though, of the content of the programs they established, and of the popularity of those programs.

48 Marion Harland (Mrs E. P. Terhune), 'Address: Cooperation and Organization Among Women for the Building Up of Homes,' at the Sixth Annual Meeting of the New York Association of Working Girls' Societies, *The Discussions of the Convention Held in New York City, 1890, and the Proceedings of the Sixth Annual Meeting of the N.Y. Association*, New York, Trow's Printing and Bookbinding Co., 1890, p. 119. Reverend Burgess of Canton, Illinois cites this comment approvingly in 'Working Women and Girls,' *Far and Near*, vol. 1, no. 5, March 1891, p. 74, adding, 'That is a simile that only a woman would have thought of.'

49 Ibid., p. 74.

50 New York Association of Working Girl's Societies, *Discussions of Convention, 1890*, p. 98. The Conventions of the Societies tended to discuss issues which had been previously explored in club talks; what are reported in various proceedings are not minutes of unstructured discussion at the Conventions, but short speeches and papers presented by directors and club members, and prepared prior to the meetings. The present paper, more informal than most, is evidently a transcription or impression of an earlier club discussion on the subject.

51 M. J., 'Married and Single Life,' pp. 18–19.

52 Cohen, op. cit., p. 303. Descriptions of her parents' attempts, and their consequences, are on pp. 201–4, 212–29, 302–3.

53 Stokes, 'No Other Thoughts' column for *Jewish Daily News*, 1903. In Rose Pastor Stokes Papers, Yale University, Box 6, file 2. Yale University, New Haven.

54 Letter from Rachel Hoffman of Chicago, 'To the Otherwise Happy,' printed in Stokes Column in the *Jewish Daily News*, 1903. Stokes Papers, Box 6, file 2. Yale University.

55 Ibid.

56 Katherine Pearson Woods, Review of Eliza Chester, *The Unmarried Woman*, New York, Dodd, Mead & Co., The Portia

Library, 1893, in *Far and Near*, vol. 3, no. 30, April 1893,
p. 124.

57 'Spinster or Relict?' (unsigned), in *Far and Near*, vol. 1, no. 12,
October 1891, p. 214.

58 Ibid.

59 M. S., 'Married and Single Life,' in Dodge, ed., *Thoughts of Busy
Girls*, pp. 25–6. This and the preceding citations involve as well
elements of a certain incipient feminism, and of women's
commitment to their work. These considerations will be dealt
with later, however.

60 Woods, Review, op. cit., p. 124; 'Spinster or Relict?', p. 214.

61 Cohen, op. cit., p. 201. After recounting these reactions, she
adds that she looked in the mirror for a long time to verify her
conclusions. She was then sixteen.

62 Anon., *Four Years*, p. 310. The anonymous author is repeating a
comment made to her by a woman with whom she had worked.
See also the 'day-dream' quote on p. 308. Also, Van Vorst and
Van Vorst, op. cit.; and Richardson, op. cit.

63 Woods and Kennedy, op. cit., pp. 53–4. See also p. 46 for
argument on Italians and Irish especially counting on children
as 'economic assets.'

64 See Peter Stearns, 'Working-Class Women in Britain, 1890–
1914,' in *Suffer and Be Still*, ed. Martha Vicinus, Bloomington,
IN, Indiana University Press, 1973, pp. 104–6; and Hoggart, op.
cit., p. 40, on working-class women's tradition of economic
sacrifice.

65 Woods and Kennedy, op. cit., p. 68. See also Clara E. Laughlin,
The Work-A-Day-Girl, New York, Fleming H. Revel Co., 1913,
pp. 92, 104.

66 Cohen, op. cit., pp. 211–12; also, p. 303.

67 'Factory Girl' in 'Tipple, Loom, and Rail: Songs of the
Industrialization of the South,' sung and played by Mike Seeger,
notes by Archie Green, Folkways Records FH 5273, 1965. See
also Francis Tamburro, 'A Tale of a Song: "The Lowell Factory
Girl," ' *Southern Exposure*, vol. 2, no. 1, Spring/Summer 1974,
pp. 42–51.

68 Cohen, op. cit., p. 74.

69 Hasanovitz, op. cit., p. 17.

70 Lemlich, in a speech at a rally held jointly by Wage Earners'
and College Equal Suffrage Leagues. Reported in June and July
issues for 1912 of *Life and Labor*, vol. II, no. 7., p. 216.

71 Hasanovitz, op. cit., p. 246.

72 Both are in New York State Factory Investigating Commission,
Fourth Report, 1915, vol. 4., Appendix VII, pp. 1577–8.

73 Mary Van Kleeck, *Artificial Flower Makers*, New York, Russell
Sage Foundation, 1913, p. 38.

74 Cohen, op. cit., p. 214.

75 Van Kleeck, op. cit., p. 36.

76 Quoted by N. Margarett Campbell in 'Organization and the Southern Woman,' *Life and Labor*, June 1920, vol. 10, no. 6, p. 163.

77 Mary Anderson, *Woman at Work*, Minneapolis, University of Minnesota Press, 1951, pp. 65–6.

78 New York Telegram, 18 June 1924. Rose Schneiderman Papers, Box A-97, folder of clippings. Tamiment Library, New York University, New York.

79 Ibid.

80 Schneiderman in letter to *Life and Labor*, May 1920, vol. 10, no. 5, p. 153.

81 See, for example, p. 126 above.

82 From an interview in the *Detroit News*, quoted in 'The Factory Girl and the Amateur Investigator,' in *Union-Labor Advocate*, vol. 9, no. 2, October 1908, p. 31.

Appendix

1 The Precis section is based on the comment presented by Sarah Eisenstein at the Second Berkshire Conference on the History of Women (Radcliffe College, October 1974) on papers by Nancy Schrom Dye ('Feminism or Unionism? The New York Women's Trade Union League and the Labor Movement,' subsequently published in *Feminist Studies*, vol. 3, no. 1/2, 1975, pp. 111–25) and Robin Miller Jacoby ('The Women's Trade Union League and American Feminism,' also published in *Feminist Studies*, vol. 3, no. 1/2, 1975, pp. 126–40), and other notes. The arguments of this section should be viewed as a set of hypotheses. The major focus on the conditions underlying the formation of consciousness, and the role of the Women's Trade Union League, reflects the context of the Berkshire Conference discussion. It also reflects my interpretations and addition of an introduction, for which I alone am responsible (H.B.). The permission of the Schlesinger Library of Radcliffe College and the Chicago Historical Society to reproduce the materials of the Documents section is gratefully acknowledged.

2 The isolation of women home workers added a further, social dimension to the cultural prohibitions on women's public and organizational activity. This social climate affected all Italian working-class women, including those who were employed outside the home. See Mary Van Kleeck, *Artificial Flower Makers*, New York, Russell Sage Foundation, 1913, pp. 34–5, 115–16; Louise C. Odencrantz, *Italian Women in Industry*, New York, Russell Sage Foundation, 1919, pp. 180–3; Annual Report (New York) Women's Trade Union League, 1907–1908, p. 11. Leonora O'Reilly Papers, box 16. Schlesinger Library, Radcliffe College.

3 The expression of this concern was frequently linked to a

nativist claim to 'superiority' in relation to immigrants. See
Mary E. J. Kelley, 'The American Working Girl and Trades
Unions,' *Far and Near*, vol. 1, no. 12, October 1891, p. 222.

4 See Joseph A. Hill, *Women in Gainful Occupations, 1870 to
1920*, Washington, DC, U.S. Government Printing Office, 1929,
pp. 10–11, 25, and 93, on the prevalence of wage-earning for
women in these industrial environments, particularly among
daughters of immigrants. Differences in the attitudes of Italian,
Russian Jewish and 'American' (native-born white) working
women are discussed in the 'Report of the New York Women's
Trade Union League to the Convention of the Women's Trade
Union League, Boston, June 1911,' *Life and Labor*, vol. 1, no. 9,
September 1911, p. 282. The conservative influence of specific
regional and occupational milieux are examined, respectively, in
N. Margaret Campbell, 'Organization and the Southern
Woman,' *Life and Labor*, vol. 10, no. 6, June 1920, p. 163, and
Helen Marot, 'Organizing Stenographers,' *Life and Labor*, vol. 2,
no. 10, October 1912, pp. 292–4.

5 John B. Andrews and W. D. P. Bliss, *History of Women in Trade
Unions*, Washington, Government Printing Office, 1911, reprint
edn, New York, ARNO Press, 1974, pp. 155–207; Louis Levine,
The Women's Garment Workers, New York, B. W. Huebsch,
1924, pp. 95–8, 106–7, 128–33, 144–67, 208–32; Alice Henry,
The Trade Union Woman, New York, D. Appleton and
Company, 1915, pp. 45–58; Gladys Boone, *The Women's Trade
Union Leagues in Great Britain and America*, New York,
Columbia University Press, 1942, pp. 64–110; U.S. Congress,
*Report on the Strike of Textile Workers in Lawrence,
Massachusetts in 1912*, 62nd Congress, 2nd Session, Senate
Document no. 870, Washington DC, Government Printing
Office, 1912; Melvyn Dubovsky, *We Shall Be All*, Chicago,
Quadrangle, 1969, pp. 263–85; and *Life and Labor*, vols 1–3,
1911–13, *passim*.

6 Levine, op. cit., pp. 54, 144, 219; Elizabeth Beardsley Butler,
Women and the Trades, New York, Russell Sage Foundation,
1909, reprint edn, New York, Arno Press, 1969, pp. 372–3;
Report of Interstate Conference, New York Women's Trade
Union League, Part 2, 28 September 1908, Leonora O'Reilly
papers, box 16; Lillian Matthews, *Women in Trade Unions in
San Francisco*, Berkeley, University of California Press, 1913,
pp. 57–8, 70, 78.

7 Rose Schneiderman with Lucy Goldthwaite, *All for One*, New
York, Paul. S. Eriksson, Inc., 1967, p. 86; Agnes Nestor,
Woman's Labor Leader, Rockford, IL, Bellevue Books, 1954,
p. 117; Matthews, op. cit., p. 70; Report of Interstate Conference,
op. cit., pp. 14–15. The important problem of the role of
neighborhood bases of collective support among working-class
women will not be considered.

8 Schneiderman, op. cit., p. 50.

9 See the plea of Chicago garment worker, Anna Rudnitsky, 'Time is Passing,' *Life and Labor*, vol. 2, no. 4, April 1912, p. 99.

10 The focus of some working-class women's groups on suffrage was not an origin of working women's feminism. Still, it was not an ungenuine concern. But this focus stemmed less from a belief in the paramount importance of the vote, than from its easy availability as a form for articulating a certain sense about themselves as women. Also, the presence of a whole movement centered on suffrage, with an extensive infrastructure, helped draw in working-class women. See Schneiderman, op. cit., p. 121. On the activities of wage-earners' suffrage leagues, see Alice Henry, *Women and the Labor Movement*, New York, Charles H. Doran, 1923, p. 120; 1909 Convention Proceedings, National Women's Trade Union League, p. 29/26, N.W.T.U.L. Headquarters' Records, Library of Congress; 'The Wage-Earners League of New York,' clipping, 1912, Leonora O'Reilly papers, box 15; 'Housemaids Join Voting League,' *Chicago Tribune*, 1 July 1913; and coverage in *Life and Labor*, June 1912, p. 88; September 1912, p. 288; November 1912, p. 344; and August 1913, p. 253.

11 See Karl Mannheim, 'The Problem of the Intelligensia,' in *Essays in the Sociology of Culture*, London, Routledge & Kegan Paul, 1956, p. 96, on the relation between confrontation with definitions developed by others and the emergence of women's group consciousness.

12 'Social feminists' included women reformers who sought to improve conditions for women and children of the working class through the social settlements, protective labor legislation, consumer education, the unionization of working women and other methods.

13 1909 Convention Proceedings, op. cit., 29/26; Schneiderman, op. cit., pp. 123–4; Pauline Newman letter to Rose Schneiderman, July 26, 1912, Rose Schneiderman papers, box A-94, Folder 1912, Tamiment Library.

14 Stella Franklin, letters to Agnes Nestor, 26 May 1916 and 21 October 1916, Agnes Nestor papers, folder 4, Chicago Historical Society; 'Tommy' (Agnes O'Brien) letter to Leonora O'Reilly, n.d., Leonora O'Reilly papers, box 6, folder 56; Pauline Newman letter to Rose Schneiderman, 1 December 1911, Rose Schneiderman papers, box A-95; Leonora O'Reilly letter of resignation from the Women's Trade Union League, to Gertrude Barnum, 29 December 1905, Leonora O'Reilly papers, box 1, folder 1, Pauline Newman letter to Rose Schneiderman, 9 February 1912, Rose Schneiderman papers, box A–94, folder 1912.

15 Rose Schneiderman, letter, in *Life and Labor*, May 1920, p. 153.

16 On the experience of the Women's Trade Union League with the

American Federation of Labor leadership, see Proceedings of the National Women's Trade Union League Conference, New York, 1915, third day, afternoon session, pp. 98–128. N.W.T.U.L. Headquarters' papers, box 13.

17 Harriet Stanton Blatch and Alma Lutz, *Challenging Years. The Memoirs of Harriet Stanton Blatch*, New York, G. P. Putnam's Sons, 1940, pp. 92–5; 'Illinois Federation of Women's Clubs, Meeting of Industrial Committee,' *Union Labor Advocate*, vol. 8, no. 8, April 1908, pp. 28–33.

18 The studies of Robin Miller Jacoby, op. cit., and Nancy Schrom Dye, op. cit., point to this conclusion.

19 In 1920 only 7 per cent of all women wage-earners, and 18 per cent of women wage-earners in manufacturing industries, belonged to labor unions. Leo Wolman, *The Growth of American Trade Unions 1888–1920*, New York, National Bureau of Economic Research, 1924, pp. 98–9, 105–6.

20 Boone, op. cit., pp. 112–14.

21 See Jacoby, op. cit., and Dye, op. cit., respectively, for these arguments.

22 The most serious consequences occurred when the League's loyalty to A.F. of L. craft affiliates (the United Textile Workers and United Garment Workers) prevented it from wholeheartedly assisting in the organization of women workers in Lawrence, Massachusetts (1912) and Chicago (1915). See Boone, op. cit., pp. 102–7; the letters of Sue Ainslie Clark, n.d., Anne Withington, 11 March 1912, and Mabel Gillespie, 11 March 1912, to Mrs. Raymond Robins, National Women Trade Union League Headquarters' Records, folder June 1911–May 1913; 'Cheap Clothes and Nasty,' *The New Republic*, 1 January 1916, pp. 217–19.

23 Mary Beard decided that Clara Lemlich was not working out well as an organizer for the Wage-Earners' Suffrage League, with the result that she would have to return to factory work. Mary Beard letter to Leonora O'Reilly, 21 July, 1912, Leonora O'Reilly papers, box 5, folder 51.

24 For a clear-sighted contemporary assessment along these lines, see the letter of Stella Franklin to Agnes Nestor, 28 May 1916. Agnes Nestor papers, folder 4. Stella Franklin recognized the positive contribution of allies (and specifically that of the autocratic Margaret Dreier Robbins) in this period in spite of their financial and organizational dominance, because working women's own organization was in its 'present weak and initial stages.'

25 Nestor, op. cit., pp. 108–11. The source for the letter is the Agnes Nestor papers, folder 3. The spelling in the letters which follow has been kept as it was in the originals.

26 Annual Report, Women's Trade Union League of New York, 1908–1909. Leonora O'Reilly papers, box 16; 'Girls to Besiege

Mme. Irene's Shop,' *The Call* (N.Y.), 4 August 1910. The source
for the letter is Leonora O'Reilly papers, box 6, folder 332.
27 Letter of Lyra E. Snow to Mrs. Alice C. Clement, 6 May 1913,
Leonora O'Reilly papers, box 9, folder 132; '10,000 March,' *New
York Times*, 4 May 1913; Blatch and Lutz, op. cit., pp. 197–9;
letter of Leonora O'Reilly to Ida Millkofsky, 12 May 1913,
Leonora O'Reilly papers, box 6, folder 53, which is also the
source for the letters of Ida Millkofsky.
28 'The Wage-Earners' League,' clipping. n.d. [1912], Leonora
O'Reilly papers, box 15.
29 'Women Invade Congress,' *New York Times*, 14 March 1912;
U.S. Senate, 'Hearings before a joint committee of the
Committee on the Judiciary and the Committee on Woman
Suffrage, on Woman Suffrage,' 62nd Congress, 3rd Session.
Document no. 1035. Washington, DC, Government Printing
Office, 1913. 84, 90–1.
30 The source for the leaflet is the Leonora O'Reilly papers, box 15.
31 'Suffrage Demanded by Working Women,' *New York Times*, 23
April, 1912. *Senators vs. Working Women*, Wage-Earners'
Suffrage League, New York, n.d., Leonora O'Reilly papers, box
15.

Afterword by Nancy F. Cott

1 See, for example, Tamara Hareven, 'Family Time and Industrial
Time; Family and Work in a Planned Corporation Town, 1900–
1924,' *Journal of Urban History*, vol. 1, May 1975; Louise A.
Tilly and Joan W. Scott, *Women, Work and Family*, New York,
Holt Rinehart & Winston, 1978; Herbert Gutman, *Work, Culture
and Society in Industrializing America*, New York, Alfred A.
Knopf, 1976; Alice Kessler-Harris, 'Where are the Organized
Women Workers?' *Feminist Studies*, vol. 3, Fall 1975, 'Organizing
the Unorganizable: Three Jewish Women and Their Union,'
Labor History, vol. 17, Winter 1976, *Out To Work: A History of
Wage-Earning Women in the U.S.*, New York, Oxford University
Press, 1982; Heidi Hartmann, 'Capitalism, Patriarchy, and Job
Segregation by Sex,' *Signs*, vol.1, Spring 1976, and special issue
of *The Review of Radical Political Economics*, vol. 8, Spring 1976.
2 Viz., Irvin Wyllie, *The Self-Made Man in America*, New
Brunswick, NJ, Rutgers University Press, 1954; Richard M.
Huber, *The American Idea of Success*, New York, McGraw-Hill,
1971; John G. Cawleti, *Apostles of the Self-Made Man: Changing
Concepts of Success in America*, University of Chicago Press,
1965; Daniel Rodgers, *The Work Ethic in Industrial America,
1850–1920*, University of Chicago Press, 1978 looks at feminist
thinking about work in one chapter, but does not attempt to
explore the point of view of working-class women.
3 Gerda Lerner, 'The Lady and the Mill Girl: Changes in the

Status of Women in the Age of Jackson, 1800–1840,' *Mid-continent American Studies Journal*, vol. 10, Spring 1969.

4 Elizabeth Pleck, 'Two Worlds in One: Work and Family,' *Journal of Social History*, vol. 10, 1977; Joan Kelly, 'The Doubled Vision of Feminist Theory,' *Feminist Studies*, vol. 5, Spring 1979; Michele Rosaldo, 'The Use and Abuse of Anthropology,' *Signs*, vol. 5, Spring 1980.

5 See Thomas Dublin, *Women at Work: The Transformation of Work and Community in Lowell, Massachusetts, 1826–1860*, New York, Columbia University Press, 1979; Scott and Tilly, *Women, Work, and Family*.

6 Leslie Woodcock Tentler, *Wage-Earning Women: Industrial Work and Family Life in the U.S., 1900–1930*, New York, Oxford University Press, 1979.

Bibliography

Abbott, Edith, *Women in Industry*, New York and London, D. Appleton and Co., 1910; reprint edn, New York, Source Book Press, 1970.

Ames, Azel, *Sex in Industry*, Boston, J. R. Osgood & Co., 1875.

Anderson, Mary, *Woman At Work*, Minneapolis, University of Minnesota Press, 1951.

Anonymous, *Four Years in the Underbrush*, New York, C. Scribner's Sons, 1921.

Ariès, Philippe, *Centuries of Childhood*, New York, Alfred A. Knopf, 1962.

Arthur, T. S. 1972, 'Sweethearts and Wives,' *Godey's Ladies Book*, December 1841, reprinted in *Root of Bitterness*, ed. Nancy F. Cott, New York, E. P. Dutton, pp. 157–70.

Ashmore, Ruth, *The Business Girl: In Every Phase of Her Life*, Philadelphia, Ladies Home Journal Library, 1895.

Bacon, Elizabeth M., 'The Growth of Household Conveniences in the United States from 1865–1900,' Unpublished PhD Thesis, Radcliffe College, 1942.

Bailyn, Lotte, 'Notes on the Role of Choice in the Psychology of Professional Women,' in *Women in America*, ed. Robert Lifton, Boston, Beacon Press, 1964.

Bendix, Reinhard, *Work and Authority in Modern Industry*, New York Harper & Row, 1963.

Benston, Margaret, 'The Political Economy of Women's Liberation,' *Monthly Review*, vol. 21, no. 4, 1969, pp. 13–27.

Betts, Lillian W., *The Leaven in a Great City*, New York, Dodd, Mead & Co., 1903.

Bosworth, Louise Marion, *The Living Wage of Women Workers*, Philadelphia, The American Academy of Political and Social Science, 1911.

Boynton, Rev. Nehemiah, 'Working Girls,' *The Arena*, vol. 2, no. 9, August 1890.

Burgess, Reverend, 'Working Women and Girls,' *Far and Near*, vol. 1, no. 5, March 1891.

Butler, Elizabeth Beardsley, *Saleswomen in Mercantile Stores*, New York, Russell Sage Foundation, 1913.

Butler, Elizabeth Beardsley, *Women and the Trades*, New York, Russell Sage Foundation, 1911; reprint edn, New York, Arno Press, 1969.

Calhoun, Arthur W., *A Social History of the American Family*, 3 vols, Cleveland, Arthur H. Clark, 1917–19.

Campbell, Helen, *Prisoners of Poverty*, Boston, Roberts Brothers, 1887; reprint edition, Westport, CT, Greenwood Press, 1970.

Campbell, Margaret, 'Organization and the Southern Woman,' *Life and Labor*, vol. 10, no. 6, June 1920.

Candee, Helen Churchill, *How Women May Earn a Living*, New York, Macmillan, 1900.

Church, Ella Rodman, *Money-Making for Ladies*, New York, Harper & Bros, 1882.

Clark, Alice, *Working Life of Women in the Seventeenth Century*, London, G. Routledge and Sons, 1919; reprint edition, New York, Augustus Kelley, 1967.

Clark, Sue Ainslie, and Wyatt, Edith, *Making Both Ends Meet*, New York, Macmillan, 1911.

Cohen, Rose, *Out of the Shadow*, New York, George Doran, 1918.

Cominus, Peter, 'Innocent Femina Sensualis in Unconscious Conflict,' in *Suffer and be Still*, ed. Martha Vicinus, Bloomington, IN, Indiana University Press, 1973.

Consumer's League of New York, *Behind the Scenes in a Restaurant*, New York, Consumer's League of New York, 1916.

Cott, Nancy F. (ed.), *Root of Bitterness*, New York, E. P. Dutton, 1972.

Crow, Duncan, *The Victorian Woman*, New York, Stein & Day, 1972.

Davies, Margery, 'The Feminization of White-Collar Occupations,' paper presented at the Second Berkshire Conference on the History of Women, Radcliffe College, 1974.

Davis, Allen F., *Spearheads for Reform*, New York, Oxford University Press, 1967.

de Koven Bowen, Louise, 'The Road to Destruction Made Easy in Chicago' in *Collected Speeches, Addresses, and Letters of Louise de Koven Bowen*, vol. I, Hull House Archives, University of Illinois at Chicago Circle, 1916.

de Tocqueville, Alexis, *Democracy in America*, 2 vols, New York, Random House, 1945.

Dodge, Grace, Outline of Address to the Girls' Friendly Societies, Brooklyn, NY, 23 January 1890, Teacher's College Archives, New York.

Dodge, Grace H. (ed.), *Thoughts of Busy Girls*, New York, Cassell Publishing Co., 1892.

Dodge, Grace H., Hunter, Thomas, Lincoln, Mrs Mary J., Packard, S. S., Palmer, Mrs A. M., Winslow, Helen M., and others, *What Women Can Earn: Occupations of Women and their Compensation*, New York, Fredrick A. Stokes. 1898.

Dutcher, Elizabeth, 'The Triangle Fire,' *Life and Labor*, August 1911, p. 265.

Dye, Nancy Schrom (1975), 'Feminism or Unionism? The New York Women's Trade Union League and the Labor Movement,' *Feminist Studies*, vol. 3, no. 1/2 (Fall), pp. 111–25.

Earle, Jaspar, *The Real Trouble and the Way Out*, Kansas City, MO, n.p., 1897.

Figes, Eva, *Patriarchal Attitudes*, New York, Stein & Day, 1970.

Flexner, Eleanor, *Century of Struggle*, Cambridge, MA, Harvard University Press, 1959.

Gans, Herbert, *The Urban Villagers*, New York, The Free Press, 1962.

Halbwachs, Maurice, *The Psychology of Social Class*, London, Heinemann, 1958.

Hamilton, Richard, *Affluence and the French Worker in the Fourth Republic*, Princeton University Press, 1967.

Hareven, Tamara, 'Women's Time, Family Time and Industrial Time: An Analysis of the Relationship of Work Careers and Family Conditions of Women Workers . . . 1910–1940,' paper presented at the Second Berkshire Conference on the History of Women, Radcliffe College, 1974.

Harland, Marion (Mrs E. P. Terhune), 'Address: Cooperation and Organization Among Women for the Building Up of Homes' at the Sixth Annual Meeting of the New York Association of Working Girls' Societies, *The Discussions of the Convention Held in New York City, 1890, and the Proceedings of the Sixth Annual Meeting of the N.Y. Association*, New York, Trow's Printing and Bookbinding Co., 1890.

Hasanovitz, Elizabeth, *One of Them, Chapters from a Passionate Autobiography*, Boston and New York, Houghton Mifflin, 1918.

Henry, Alice, *The Trade Union Woman*, New York and London, D. Appleton & Co. 1915.

Hinchey, Maggie, Speech reported in *Life and Labor*, July 1912.

Hobsbawm, Eric, 'Class Consciousness in History' in *Aspects of History and Class Consciousness*, ed. István Mészaros, London, Routledge and Kegan Paul for the Merlin Book Club, 1971.

Hoerle, Helen C., and Saltzberg, Florence B., *The Girl and the Job*, New York, Henry Holt & Co., 1919.

Hoggart, Richard, *The Uses of Literacy*, Boston, Beacon Press, 1961.

Horton, John, 'Order and Conflict Theories of Social Problems as Competing Ideologies,' *American Journal of Sociology*, vol. 71, no. 5, 1966, pp. 701–13.

Hyman, Herbert, 'The Value Systems of Different Classes,' in *Class*,

Status and Power, ed. R. Bendix and S. M. Lipset, 2nd edn, New York, The Free Press, 1966.

Jacoby, Robin Miller, 'The Women's Trade Union League and American Feminism', *Feminist Studies*, vol. 3, no. 1/2, 1975, Fall, pp. 126–40.

Jones, Mary H., *Autobiography of Mother Jones*, Chicago, Charles H. Kerr & Co., 1925.

Josephson, Hannah, *The Golden Threads*, New York, Duell, Sloan & Pearce, 1949.

Komarovsky, Mirra, *Blue Collar Marriage*, New York, Vintage Books, 1967.

Korsch, Karl, *Karl Marx*, London, Chapman & Hall, 1938; reprint edn, New York, Russell & Russell, 1963.

Kraditor, Aileen, *Ideas of the Woman Suffrage Movement, 1890–1920*, New York, Columbia University Press, 1965.

Larcom, Lucy, *A New England Girlhood*, Boston, Houghton Mifflin, 1889; reprint edn, New York, Arno Press, 1974.

Laselle, Mary A., and Whiley, Katherine E., *Vocations for Girls*, Boston, New York, Chicago, Houghton Mifflin, 1913.

Laughlin, Clara E., *The Work-A-Day-Girl*, New York, Fleming H. Revell Co., 1913.

Lemisch, Jesse, 'Towards a Democratic History,' Ann Arbor, MI, Radical Education Project publication, 1968.

Lemlich, Clara, Speech reported in *Life and Labor*, vol. II, no. 7., July, 1912.

Lerner, Gerda, *The Grimke Sisters from South Carolina*, New York, Schocken Books, 1969.

Lerner, Gerda, 'The Lady and the Mill Girl: Changes in the Status of Women in the Age of Jackson,' *Midcontinent American Studies Journal*, vol. 10, no. 1, 1969, pp. 5–15.

Levine, Louis, *The Women's Garment Workers*, New York, B. W. Huebsch, 1924; reprint edn, New York, Arno Press, 1969.

Lilenthal, Meta Stern, *From Fireside to Factory*, New York, Rand School, 1916.

MacLean, Annie Marian, *The Wage-Earning Woman*, New York, Macmillan, 1910.

MacLean, Annie Marion, *Women Workers and Society*, Chicago, A. C. McClurg & Co., 1916.

Mannheim, Karl, *Ideology and Utopia*, New York and London, Harcourt, Brace, Jovanovich, 1936.

Mannheim, Karl, 'On the Nature of Economic Ambition and its Significance for the Social Education of Man' in *Essays on the Sociology of Knowledge*, London, Routledge & Kegan Paul, 1952.

Mannheim, Karl, 'On the Problem of Generations,' in *Essays on the Sociology of Knowledge*, London, Routledge & Kegan Paul, 1952.

Mannheim, Karl, 'The Problem of the Intelligentsia' in *Essays on the Sociology of Culture*, London, Routledge & Kegan Paul, 1956.

Marcus, Steven, *The Other Victorians*, New York, Vintage, 1964.

Marcuse, Herbert, *One-Dimensional Man*, Boston, Beacon Press, 1964.

Marx, Karl, and Engels, Frederick, 'The German Ideology,' in *Writings of the Young Marx on Philosophy and Society*, ed. Lloyd D. Easton and Kurt H. Guddat, Garden City, NY, Anchor Books, 1967.

Matthews, Lillian, *Women in Trade Unions in San Francisco*, Berkeley, University of California Press, 1913.

Meyer, Annie Nathan (ed.), *Woman's Work in America*, New York, Henry Holt & Co., 1891; reprint edition, New York, Arno Press, 1972.

Michels, Robert, 'The Origins of the Anti-Capitalist Mass Spirit,' trans. Kurt Shell, in *Man in Contemporary Society: A Sourcebook*, ed. Contemporary Civilization Staff, Columbia College, vol. I, New York, Columbia University Press, 1955.

Miller, Walter, 'Lower Class Cultures as a Generating Milieu of Gang Delinquency,' *Journal of Social Issues*, vol. 14, no. 3, 1958, pp. 5–19.

Neff, Wanda, *Victorian Working Women*, London, Allen & Unwin, 1929.

Nestor, Agnes, *Woman's Labor Leader*, Rockford, IL, Bellevue Books, 1954.

O'Neill, William, *Everyone Was Brave*, Chicago, Quadrangle Books, 1969.

Orenstein, Marie S., 'How the Working Girl of New York City Lives' in State of New York Factory Investigating Commission, *Fourth Report of the Factory Investigation Commission, 1915*, vol. IV, 1915, Albany, pp. 1700–1.

Papashvily, Helen Waite, *All the Happy Endings*, New York, Harper & Row, 1956.

Parkin, Frank, *Class Inequality and Political Order*, New York and Washington, Praeger, 1971.

Parsons, Talcott, 'Age and Sex in the Social Structure of the U.S.,' in *Essays in Sociological Theory*, rev. edn, Chicago, The Free Press, 1954.

Parsons, Talcott, 'An Approach to the Sociology of Knowledge' in *The Sociology of Knowledge*, ed. James E. Curtis and John W. Petras, New York and Washington, Praeger, 1970.

Perry, Lorinda, *Millinery as a Trade For Women*, New York, Longman, 1916.

Petersen, M. Jeanne, 'The Victorian Governess: Status Incongruence in Family and Society,' in *Suffer and be Still*, ed. Martha Vicinus, Bloomington, IN, University of Indiana Press, 1973.

Pinchbeck, Ivy, *Women Workers and the Industrial Revolution 1750–1850*, London, Routledge & Kegan Paul, 1930; reprint edn, New York, Augustus Kelley, 1969.

Richardson, Dorothy, *The Long Day: The Story of a New York*

Working Girl, New York, The Century Co., 1905; reprinted in *Women at Work*, ed. William O'Neill, New York, New York Times Books, 1972.

Rossi, Alice, 'Equality between the Sexes: an Immodest Proposal,' in *Women in America*, ed. Robert Lifton, Boston, Beacon Press, 1964.

Rossi, Alice (ed.), *The Feminist Papers*, New York, Bantam, 1973.

Rotella, Elyce, 'Occupational Segregation: A Case Study of American Clerical Workers, 1870–1930,' paper presented at the Second Berkshire Conference on the History of Women, Radcliffe College, 1974.

Ryan, Mary, 'American Society and the Cult of Domesticity, 1830–1860,' Unpublished PhD Thesis, University of California at Santa Barbara, 1971.

Schneiderman, Rose, with Goldthwaite, Lucy, *All For One*, New York, Paul S. Eriksson, 1967.

Scott, Joan, and Tilly, Louise, 'Daughters, Wives, Mothers, Workers: Peasants and Working Class Women in the Transition to an Industrial Economy in France,' paper presented at the Second Berkshire Conference on the History of Women, Radcliffe College, 1974.

Simkhovich, Mary Kingsbury, 'A New Social Adjustment,' in *Proceedings of the Academy of Political Science, vol. 1, The Economic Position of Women*, New York, The Academy of Political Science, Columbia University.

Sinclair, Andrew, *The Emancipation of American Women*, New York, Harper & Row, 1966.

Smith, Judith, 'The "New Woman" Knows How to Type: Some Connections between Sexual Ideology and Clerical Work, 1890–1930,' paper presented at the Second Berkshire Conference on the History of Women, Radcliffe College, 1974.

Smith, Page, *Daughters of the Promised Land*, Boston, Little, Brown, 1970.

Smuts, Robert, *Women and Work in America*, New York, Columbia University Press, 1959.

'Spinster or Relict?' (Unsigned), *Far and Near*, vol. 1, no. 12, October, 1891, p. 214.

Stanton, Elizabeth Cady, *Eighty Years and More*, New York, T. Fisher Unwin, 1898; reprint edn, New York, Schocken Books, 1971.

Stearns, Peter, 'Working-Class Women in Britain, 1890–1914,' in *Suffer and be Still*, ed. Martha Vicinus, Bloomington, IN, Indiana University Press, 1973.

Stein, Leon, *The Triangle Fire*, Philadelphia and New York, J. B. Lippincott, 1962.

Stokes, Rose Pastor, 'No Other Thoughts' column for *Jewish Daily News*, 1903.

Tamburro, Francis, 'A Tale of a Song; "The Lowell Factory Girl," '
   Southern Exposure, vol. 2, no. 1, Spring/Summer, 1974, pp. 42–51.
Taylor, Mabel, 'Where the Men are to Blame,' *Life and Labor*, June
   1921.
Thompson, E. P., *The Making of the English Working Class*, New
   York, Vintage, 1963.
Thompson, E. P., 'Time, Work-Discipline, and Industrial
   Capitalism,' *Past and Present*, no. 38, 1967, pp. 56–97.
'Tipple, Loom, and Rail: Songs of the Industrialization of the South,'
   Sung and played by Mike Seeger, notes by Archie Green,
   Folkways Records FH 5273, 1965.
Van Kleeck, Mary, *Artificial Flower Makers*, New York, Russell
   Sage Foundation, 1913.
Van Vorst, Mrs John and Van Vorst, Marie, *The Woman Who
   Toils. Being the Experience of Two Gentlewomen as Factory Girls*,
   New York, Doubleday, Page & Co., 1903.
Vicinus, Martha (ed.), *Suffer and Be Still*, Bloomington, IN, Indiana
   University Press, 1973.
Walkowitz, Daniel, 'Working-Class Women in the Gilded Age:
   Factory, Community and Family Life Among Cohoes, New York,
   Cotton Workers,' *Journal of Social History*, vol. 5, no. 4, 1972,
   pp. 464–90.
Weaver, E. W., *Profitable Vocations for Girls*, New York and
   Chicago, A. S. Barnes Co., 1916.
Weber, Max, 'Class, Status, Party,' in *From Max Weber*, ed. H. H.
   Gerth and C. Wright Mills, New York, Oxford University Press,
   1958.
Welter, Barbara, 'The Cult of True Womanhood,' *American
   Quarterly*, vol. 18, no. 2, 1966, pp. 151–74.
Women's Educational and Industrial Union, Department of
   Research, in co-operation with the Massachusetts Department of
   Health, *The Food of Working Women in Boston*, Lucille Eaves,
   director, Boston, Women's Educational and Industrial Union,
   1917.
Woods, Katherine Pearson, Review of Eliza Chester, *The
   Unmarried Woman*, New York, Dodd, Mead & Co., The Portia
   Library, in *Far and Near*, vol. 3, no. 30, April 1893, p. 124.
Woods, Robert A., and Kennedy, Albert J., *Young Working Girls*,
   Boston and New York, Houghton Mifflin, 1913.
'Working Women,' *New York Sun*, 14 November 1863.
Yans-McLaughlin, Virginia, 'Patterns of Work and Family
   Organization: Buffalo's Italians,' *The Journal of Interdisciplinary
   History*, vol. 2, no. 2, 1971, pp. 299–314.

Index